BRAND NEW

Brand New is a powerful tool that will anchor and establish any believer more deeply in their faith. Some books look great on a bookshelf, but this book makes its best appearance in the fruit that it produces in the life of any hungry reader. Les Beauchamp is a prototype pastor who is led by the Great Shepherd, Jesus Christ, and who, in turn, is passionate about leading others into green pastures. I am excited to see how God will use this book and its message to help others live *brand new lives!*

LEE CUMMINGS — Senior Pastor of Radiant Church, Kalamazoo, MI; Overseer of Radiant Network and Author of *Be Radiant* and *FLOURISH*

Pastor Les has been my friend and colleague for 30 years. His love for God and people is reflected in his ministry service. His passion to see people introduced into a loving relationship with God has been consistent for all the years I have known him and is reflected in the labor of love this book represents!

If you're the person coming *brand new* into God's forever family, it can be intimidating and overwhelming and could even discourage you from thinking about becoming a part. This can be especially tough for those who grew up in broken or unhealthy families.

That is what I love about this book. It is a healthy introduction to the family of God. If you have come into the family through an encounter with Jesus, we celebrate this, but now what? How do you become a vital part and learn the values, culture, language and mission of the family?

Brand New is the *Cliffs Notes* you need to gain an understanding of the necessary foundations of godly living as you take your first steps as a member of God's own family. Oh, how I wish I would have had this book when I first became a *brand new* follower of Jesus.

Use this book as a tool and as a gift to help you in your journey with God! Welcome to the family!

TOM LANE — Apostolic Senior Pastor; Gateway Church, Southlake, TX

Pastor Les is passionate about pointing people to Jesus in a kind, caring and generous way. His gentleness is evident throughout *Brand New* as he walks a new Christ-follower through the foundations of their new-found faith. Throughout this resource, there are many great analogies and stories to help the reader easily comprehend complex truths. This book is such a gift, and all church leaders would do well to include it as part of their assimilation process. I highly recommend it.

JOSEPH SANGL — President and CEO, INJOY Stewardship Solutions; Author of *I Was Broke. Now I'm Not, Oxen* and *What Everybody Should Know About Money Before They Enter the REAL WORLD*

Brand New is an encouraging, engaging book overflowing with grace and guidance. Les Beauchamp's practical wisdom and exercises provide clarity in developing your relationship with Christ and direction in living as an accepted, loved, forgiven and peace-filled Christ-follower. This exceptional book reaffirms your decision to fully surrender to Jesus, provides simple disciplines for continual spiritual growth and challenges you to leave a lasting impact in the world. This is truly an affirming book you'll go back to again and again.

AMIE GAMBOIAN — Executive Leadership Coach

I'm highly privileged to know the author of *this* book. He's my friend, Les. I'm even more privileged to know the author of *THE* book. He's my Savior, Jesus. If you read my friend's book about my Savior, I think you'll experience what it means to feel *brand new.*

REV. DR. MARK P. ZEHNDER — Senior Pastor, Director of Ministries, King of Kings Church, Omaha, NE

Finally! A book that takes the spiritual foundations of our faith and unpacks them in a clear and meaningful way for seekers as well as for the spiritually mature. If the mandate to make disciples of all nations is going to be taken seriously, then it is resources like Pastor Les' *Brand New* that will help us fulfill the Great Commission. This is a must-read!

PASTOR MYRON PIERCE — Lead Pastor, Mission Church, Omaha, NE

The gift of life is way too precious to be buried in disorientation. So how much more precious is the gift of new life in Christ! *Brand New* is Pastor Les' gift of a "Welcome Orientation Kit" to all newcomers into the Kingdom of Jesus' Lordship.

Pastor Les' remarkably straightforward instructions describe a biblically sound and Christ-centered map and compass (two in one!) that provide life-giving orientation into your *brand new* life and how and where to go from here.

Brand New is the best guide to a new life in Jesus that I have come across in my 47 years of studying, teaching at the seminary level and living and modeling evangelism and missions. It's a must-read for every person considering a relationship with Jesus and for every person who has surrendered to His loving leadership.

DR. DIMITRIJE POPADIC — Founder and President of the Protestant Theological Seminary, Novi Sad, Serbia; Church Planter Lifegate Novi Sad Campus Pastor

Les Beauchamp is a friend and powerful leader in the city of Omaha where we both serve. His teaching is impactful; his passion is contagious, and his ability to make spiritual truths come alive is profound. *Brand New* is packed with powerful truths I wish every Christ-follower would read, understand and live. Whether you're a seasoned follower of Christ or just beginning your journey, *Brand New* will help you establish and strengthen your walk with God.

RON DOTZLER — Founder and Chairman of the Board of Abide Network, Omaha, NE

Reading *Brand New* is like sitting down with a friend over coffee. Les makes no assumptions of his readers and conversationally walks them through a summary of the Christian life weaving together Scripture, helpful illustrations and his own journey.

PASTOR GAVIN JOHNSON — City Light Church, Omaha, NE

For over 25 years, I've had the privilege of pastoring a different church in the same city as Les. This has given me a front-row seat to watch God use him to help reach people that need Jesus. *Brand New* is the perfect tool for every new Christian to take the next step of discovery in a lifelong relationship with the Maker of the universe. It is biblically sound, practical and conversational. A must-have for your growth journey!

GARY HOYT — Lead Pastor, Bellevue Christian Center, Omaha, NE

BRAND NEW
LIVING AS GOD'S NEW CREATION

Les Beauchamp

Brand New: Living as God's New Creation
© 2019 Les Beauchamp

ISBN 978-0-578-45163-3

Dedicated to each new creation in Christ.
May you remain faithfully His.

Cover Design & Illustrations:
DayCloud Studios – Liz Hunt, Ross Finocchiaro

Layout & Book Design:
Creative Gal LLC – Kelly M. Vaughan

Proofing & Editing:
Corie Hansen, Ryan Long, Jim Deese

Creative Direction & Publishing:
Lifegate Church – Blake Beauchamp, Amber Francis

TABLE OF CONTENTS

YOUR DECISION

YOUR GROWTH

YOUR IMPACT

FOREWORD

Receiving Christ and becoming a new creation, becoming *brand new,* is a bit like sky diving; there is a rush of adrenaline once you pluck up the courage to jump and begin hurtling through the air at 150 miles an hour. It is heaven (at least for *some* earthlings)! But then you pull the cord; your parachute deploys, and soon you are back on terra firma.

It was a great ride, but now what? This could describe the experience of many who "pray the prayer." But then life often seems to continue in much the same way as before. The problem? They have not discovered the joy of living *brand new* on a daily basis.

I have known and worked closely with Pastor Les for over 25 years, and anyone who does so quickly realizes that he is passionate about helping others experience the salvation and *brand new* life Jesus offers. However, one cannot lead a church of several thousand (plus its multiple congregations) without inevitably being swamped by a multitude of other tasks: pastoral problems of every kind, administration, strategy meetings, team meetings, numerous prayer meetings and sermon preparation— not to mention responsibilities as a husband, father and grandfather. (Les, despite his *fun loving* youthfulness, is actually a grandfather several times over!) Thus, inevitably, with such responsibilities, for many Christian leaders, helping others enter a relationship with Jesus and grow as His followers becomes something those leaders teach and preach about, but because of time pressure, end up neglecting in their own personal lives.

And, in this, Les is unique among the hundreds of Christian leaders I have known over the last 50 years. Whether it is at Starbucks, the dry cleaners, Chick-fil-A or the gym, Les simply can't stop gossiping the gospel (and often personally walking with those who respond) – despite his overwhelming responsibilities within the church. And this is what uniquely qualifies him to write this book; *he practices what he preaches—* it is in his DNA and burns like a fire in his heart.

It is out of this lifestyle of passionate proclamation that this book came to be written. There are many books for "seekers" and even more, both long and short, theological and basic, that explain salvation by faith in Christ and how to receive Jesus personally, but few unpack what being a new creation *actually means*.

If you are in the process of seeking to understand who Jesus is and what is involved in following Him, then this book is for you! If you are struggling to get free from bondage and addiction, this book will break your chains. If you have decided to follow Jesus but are confused by words like *justification* and *regeneration* and by terms like "born again," this will make these pivotal (but often complex) truths transparent. If you have already given your life to Jesus but are unsure about joining a community of Christians (a church), this book will explain why doing so (immediately!) is crucial. If you have heard that the Holy Spirit can empower your life in extraordinary ways (and keep you *brand new!*), but have no idea of how, this book will become your GPS. If you want to learn how to pray joyfully and persistently (and see answers!), this book will guide you. If you have discovered that sharing your new-found faith is central to following Jesus, but doing so scares you to death, *then start by simply giving this book to your friends.* If you want to know how the Bible can come alive and become your daily bread, this book can become the key to unlock it.

There is no shortage of Christian books available, but this is one you not only should buy and read for yourself; you also should purchase multiple copies and give them away. Let me explain why . . .

If I could recommend only one book to read (and give away!) to someone who is seeking to find and follow Jesus, *Brand New* would be it!

RAY MAYHEW

Former Church Planter, Leadership Trainer in the UK and Middle East; Biblical Studies Pastor, Lifegate Church; Current writer, instructor and mentor for church-planting workers with the Antioch Movement, Waco, TX

INTRODUCTION

*Whoever is a believer in Christ is a **new creation.**
The old way of living has disappeared. A new way
of living has come into existence.*
II Corinthians 5:17 GW [emphasis added]

Although it was December, the night was unusually hot and muggy as I walked back home from the cab station. At the time, I was living in the town of Tsoying, on the island of Taiwan. I'd just left the home of a friend who told me the story (again) of how he had discovered a ***brand new*** life by trusting Jesus fully. All my arguments as to why I thought this wasn't possible were beginning to crumble in the face of the compelling, consistent story of how his life had drastically changed for the better.

Over the last six months of our friendship, I had given him every reason why a person should have to "be good" in order to go to heaven and "earn their way" through good deeds. I tried to give myself a pass with excuses like: *I'm only human and not that bad of a person.*

Can any of you relate to this?

Lack of peace and purpose, overwhelming guilt, the facade of control I thought I had, these all gripped me. But I could not escape the truth my friend kept repeating: No one is good enough, and that's why God has to give us a **brand new** life through the gift of His son, Jesus.

I wanted that life but was afraid. What if I blew it? What if I didn't measure up? What if none of this was real?

These questions and conflicting thoughts swirled in my head as I made my way home late that night. I'd lost all confidence that what I believed about God, life, and eternity could result in my forgiveness, freedom and eternal life after I died. I wanted what my friend Doug had: assurance, real peace and a changed life.

When I closed the door to my room, I felt a chill, perhaps from the AC unit that hummed in the window, but perhaps it was more than that. I knew I'd come to a crossroads and had to make a decision.

And then, the truth, it hit me like a freight train. I was guilty as charged. A pain stabbed sharply in my heart, and the words in my head overwhelmed me: "It's time to stop playing God. You are not God and never will be. You are not in control. You've blown it. It's time to confess you are guilty and in need of forgiveness. It's time to surrender to My Love."

Was this God talking, or me talking? It didn't matter. It was true.

I felt such guilt, and the weight seemed to press me down until my knees hit the cold, hard, terrazzo floor. Like a dam breaking open, words of confession and commitment came flooding out of my mouth, "I am not good. I am guilty. I can't be good enough. Have mercy on me, God. If you could find it in Your heart to forgive me, I will follow you and serve you all the days of my life. I put my trust in Jesus alone. Change my life. Amen."

Calm.

Peace filled my room. I wasn't sure what had just happened, but I was sure of my commitment. I went to bed.

When I woke up, my first thought went to what I had done the night before. Was it real?

I parted my curtains and was stunned by what I saw. It was as if all my life an oily, dirty film had covered my eyes, and now the sun, the trees, the birds gleamed in unfiltered beauty. What was blurry was now clear, pristine, and startling. What was black and white, was now color. Not sure what was happening, I walked down the hallway of our home and saw my mother (who, by the way, had told me many times about Jesus; we had argued often, and I was living in a state of anger and frustration toward her). The moment I laid eyes on her, I was shocked by the love that flooded my heart.

What's going on? What happened to the old me? The angry, judgmental, hateful me?

He was gone. I had become a new creation, as the Bible verse at the beginning declares. I was **BRAND NEW!** And I was about to discover a life I could not even begin to imagine.

Since that December night, in 1976, God's presence has been more real to me and His plans more fulfilling with each passing year.

If you've read this far, it's most likely you have made a similar decision to entrust your life fully to Jesus. Or maybe you are curious about His life, teachings and startling claims.

If you've made that decision, congratulations and welcome to a *brand new* life!

If you're still on a path of discovery, don't stop.

Now, I had the huge advantage of having my friend Doug help me understand and grow in my faith. I still believe this is the best way to grow as God's "new creation." However, not everybody has such a friend. The book you hold in your hands was written for you in order to help you experience fully, and understand more clearly, the amazing change that has just happened to you. It's designed to progressively move you through the basics of faith and to help you experience the life of ongoing forgiveness, freedom, peace, and purpose found only in a personal, daily relationship with Jesus. You can read it on your own or together with another follower of Jesus so that you can talk about it.

I've purposely written for people who are just beginning this brand new life but also for those who don't have someone to answer their questions, pray with them and help them get to know Jesus more. I'm praying for you and asking God to begin the process of growing you into the person He's always destined you to be.

Let's begin with an amazing verse from the Bible. It's a promise from God to you and me about His plans for those who choose to follow Him!

> *"For I know the plans I have for you," declares the Lord, "plans to prosper you and not to harm you, plans to give you a hope and a future."*
> Jeremiah 29:11 NIV

"For I know the plans I have for you," declares the Lord, "plans to prosper you and not to harm you, plans to give you a hope and a future."

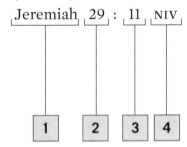

UNDERSTANDING SCRIPTURE REFERENCES

If you are not familiar with the Bible, the "Jeremiah 29:11 NIV" notation may not make sense. To help find our way around Scripture, we use what is called a Bible reference.

For example, this reference breaks down like this:

1. The **book**, or section of the Bible, is *Jeremiah*.
2. The **chapter** in Jeremiah is *29*.
3. The **verse**, within the chapter, is *11*.
4. The **translation** is *NIV* which stands for New International Version. There are many translations. You've probably heard of the King James Version (KJV) which is the one with all the "thees" and "thous." I don't speak that way anymore, dost thou? The different translations help us read the Bible in the common language of the people which has been God's desire from the start. I'll use a variety of translations which I hope will be easier for you to understand because they are up to date with modern language.

The above breakdown goes for all Bible references. One verse you may see held up at football games is "John 3:16." To look it up in the Bible, go to the book of John, the third chapter and the sixteenth verse. I hope this helps.

I didn't really understand the Bible when I chose to follow Jesus. I hope that is a comfort to you as you read. Learning to "get" the Bible is a journey that takes time. The Bible is a love letter (granted, a big one) written to those God loves. Until we choose to love God and let Him love us, we can never completely understand this love letter. The Bible actually says that when we trust Jesus completely, we experience a metamorphosis (like a creepy caterpillar becoming a gorgeous monarch butterfly), a rebirth into the person God always has meant us to be.

Let's look at our starting verse again:

> Whoever is a believer in Christ is a **new creation.** The old way of living has disappeared. A new way of living has come into existence.
> II Corinthians 5:17 GW [emphasis added]

This verse tells us that when we let go of our way and choose Jesus' way, we become a new creation! I didn't have those words to describe what happened to me when I knelt on the floor of my room in 1976. But when I made a commitment to Jesus, something did happen! I wasn't the same person. A new-me was birthed inside: same skin, different person. I no longer wanted to live for myself.

LIVING WHAT YOU'RE LEARNING

Have you ever read a book with so much to say that, by the time you finished, you couldn't remember half of it? To help you not have that experience at the end of this book, you'll find me stopping periodically at sections I've called *Living What You're Learning*. These are opportunities to apply what you've read. And I believe that, by doing so, you'll find these truths will become part of your everyday life.

When you reach these sections, try taking a moment wherever you are: a library, coffee shop, booth in a bar, your room, your desk, your car, and ask God to begin to teach you about living this brand new life as a follower of Jesus. You can ask (pray) silently or out loud if you want. Use your own words or repeat these:

PRAYER

God, I know you are at work in my life. That's why I'm reading this book. I want to learn what it means to be a follower of Jesus. I'm new at this. I need your help. Thanks. Amen!

(By the way, *amen* means, "may it be so!" or "that's what's up!")

YOUR DECISION

CHAPTER 1
WHAT MAKES JESUS SO UNIQUE?

I ran into a man named John at Walmart's tire section. He told me that he used to come to the church where I pastor. "Used to come" always gets my attention, so I asked why he no longer attended. His answer was, "I'm fed up with hypocrites, so I decided to change religions and found one where they have regular potluck meals."

I couldn't hear you as you read that last sentence, but I imagine you said something like, "What?!!" John missed the most important reality of our spiritual life. It's not about where you go to church; it's about who you go to for life.

And it's definitely not about potluck meals.

Have you ever found yourself saying, "It doesn't matter who you worship as long as you're sincere. Aren't all religions really the same anyway?"

I believe that statement to be partly, but not wholly, true. Some of the most dangerous untruths are actually partial truths. Let me explain. All the world's religions from Buddhism, to Islam, to Hinduism, to Judaism, to Paganism offer a way to God that hinges on religious ritual, performance or particular lifestyle to earn a better existence now and to hopefully secure a comfy hammock in the afterlife. Words like *heaven, eternal moksha, paradise, transcendence, oneness with the universe* and *nirvana* are only a few terms used to describe the final goal of religion. Each has its teachers, leaders, prophets and founders who show people the way they should live. And every religion believes in some form of judgment, reckoning or karma.

- Religion is about **doing** the law, the ritual or alms in order to be virtuous.

- Religion is about **being on a path** that leads to God, peace and heaven.

- Religion is about **trying to make up for** our bad deeds by doing good deeds.

- Religion is about **hoping you'll make it** in the end but never being sure (Proverbs 14:12).

Here is where things shift when it comes to Jesus and why "all religions are the same" is <u>not</u> the whole truth. Following Jesus isn't meant to be a religion at all.

Following Jesus is a Relationship.

- Jesus didn't come to help us be good enough. He came because none of us *are* good enough to pass the judgment, or reckoning, for the many ways we've blown it with God and others in this life.

- Jesus didn't come <u>to **show** us the way</u> to life but <u>to **be** the way</u> so that we could follow Him (John 14:6).

- Jesus came to die on the cross and pay the guilt and punishment for our bad deeds (Isaiah 53:6).

- Jesus came so that we could have a personal relationship with God through faith in Him and have the assurance of life eternal.

Religion says, "**DO** and hope it's good enough." Jesus says, "**DONE.** What I did for you on the cross has made you good enough." His death and His resurrection have cleansed us completely for our wrongs and provided a way to relationship and eternal life for all who put their trust in Him. It is not what you do; it is who you know and follow (John 17:3; Hebrews 4:15).

Jesus isn't just a religious figure. He's not just a good teacher. He wasn't just a good man. He's not one of many optional gods of Hinduism.

Jesus **IS** God and calls every person to follow Him.

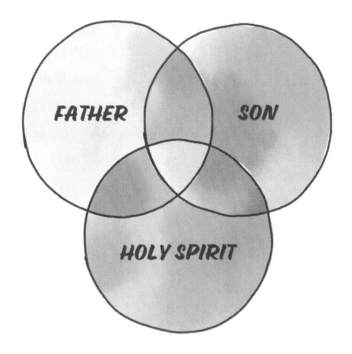

Now, before I unpack who Jesus is a bit more (and what makes Him totally unique), I have to tell you about a word you may have heard before: "the Trinity." Whoa! Don't let that word shut you down. I know it may sound a bit like religious code or something, but it's actually a word that describes a reality which, although a HUGE mystery, is true.

Are you ready for this?

There is one true and living God, and He chooses to express Himself in three separate beings, all at the same time! I know, wild, isn't it?! But it's true. The first hint we get about God being One, but also more than One, is in the first book of the Bible when God creates humanity:

> Then God said, "Let us make humans
> in <u>our</u> image, in our likeness."
> Genesis 1:26 GW

Why is this so important, you might ask? Because if you don't know this, you might get confused as you learn more about Jesus. In the Bible, God reveals Himself to us as:

God the Father (Luke 3:22)
God the Son/Jesus (Hebrews 1:1–3)
God the Holy Spirit (John 14:26).

I've found staying simple helps me understand things that are complex. H_2O. Water. This compound can be revealed as ice, steam, and liquid, and, at the same time, it is still water. An apple is made up of skin, fruit and seeds that all have different functions and, yet, are still the same apple. God reveals Himself as Father, Son and Holy Spirit but, at the same time, is still one God. If the most essential compound on Earth, or something as common as an apple can be one, but have three expressions, is it possible that the Creator of water and apples can be one, yet expressed in three persons?

I know, mind blowing! Being aware of the Trinity is important if we are to see how unique Jesus is among all the religious teachers and leaders of the world's religions. He is the unique expression of God that we could see, hear and touch. He walked on Earth so we could know what walking with Him daily is like. If you want to talk about being unique, this is huge.

As I said, this is a mystery, but it helps to think about it as you start to read the Bible and find yourself asking, "Which one of these three is God?" The answer is, they all "is" God since there is but one God (not good grammar, but good news).

LIVING WHAT YOU'RE LEARNING
We've just tackled two truths which may be completely new to you.
1. Following Jesus is a relationship, not a religion.
2. God is the Trinity: one God expressing Himself in three persons at the same time.

Take time to go back and read this again. Then spend a minute or two thanking God that because of Jesus' offer of life, you don't have to be on the religious hamster wheel anymore.

Let's talk about three BIG ideas that further describe Jesus' uniqueness.

1. JESUS IS GOD, COMING TO US BEFORE WE COULD EVER COME TO HIM

God was so concerned for the state of our lives that rather than sending a message to help us, He sent Himself, Jesus, as a human to live with us, heal us, teach us and call us to follow Him. He wasn't born into a privileged family. He was born into poverty. He wasn't drawn to those who had it all together. He pursued those who knew they didn't have it all together. He didn't come to establish a system of behavior to get us to God. He came to offer Himself as the only one who could rescue us from our destructive choices.

> *For God so loved the world that He gave His only Son. Whoever puts his trust in God's Son will not be lost but will have life that lasts forever. For God did not send His Son into the world to say it is guilty. He sent His Son so the world might be saved from the punishment of sin by Him.*
> John 3:16–17 NLV

God sent His Son into the world and into whatever state you find yourself in. Jesus doesn't ask you to clean up your act and then follow Him. He invites each of us to put our full trust in Him alone so He can bring light into the dark areas of our lives and begin our great transformation into a new creation, a person His very own.

2. JESUS IS GOD'S SON, DYING IN OUR PLACE TO FORGIVE US

Can you think of any word in the English language that strikes more fear than *cancer?*

After my wife was diagnosed, not once, but twice, with breast cancer, she and I experienced the fear that cancer brings. With the discovery of cancer in her body, we began a difficult and painful battle for her life. After a double mastectomy, numerous other surgeries, chemo and radiation, by God's kindness, my wife came through it alive. But it wasn't a given that she would survive. Instead, it demanded our willingness to listen to experts, do whatever was necessary and trust God through the entire ordeal.

Why am I bringing up cancer? Because nothing else I know of in the physical world so parallels the reality of a malignant, terminal, spiritual cancer that has infected every human being on our planet. This cancer, the Bible calls **sin**. I know, you've heard that word so many times and in so many contexts, from talk show hosts making light of the concept, to the mouths of rabid, so-called "Christians" who don't act Christian at all. You may prefer never to hear the word again.

However, avoiding the word *sin* and the concept, because of inaccurate and biased views, would be like avoiding an oncologist and then having an accountant diagnose the lump in your neck. When the Bible says *sin,* it helps me realize that it's talking about malignant, spiritual cancer.

Sin is cancer of the soul and spirit. It is at work to destroy God's original design of peace, purpose and relationship with Him. Sin is always terminal (Romans 5:12).

Sin is spiritual cancer.

This spiritual cancer entered the human race when Earth's first parents, Adam and Eve, made a decision to break relationship with their Creator and live for themselves, not for God and one another. Their sin entered the spiritual DNA that every single person inherits at birth. By default, we are born with a spiritual cancer gene. We then go astray by putting our trust in ourselves and seeking our own way. The spiritual cancer then spreads with each decision we make to focus on ourselves and not on God. I often remind myself that this is why *sin* is spelled with "I" in the center.

Sin is putting myself first,
before God and others.

Most all religions in the world also recognize this spiritual cancer and try to treat it with writings and rules that demand good behavior, with the hope that it will be enough to outweigh the effects of sin.

No person will be made right with God by doing what
the Law says. The Law shows us how sinful we are.
Romans 3:20 NLV

This passage shows us our tendency to wrongly treat spiritual cancer by trying to be good (doing what the law says). The real purpose of the law, which God gave to the people in the Bible and to us (i.e. the Ten Commandments, etc.), is actually to diagnose spiritual cancer, proving we have blown it over and over and are in need of a cure.

Not sure yet if you believe all this? Ask yourself two simple questions: Have you ever been selfish in thought or word or deed? Have you ever felt guilty afterward? I know I have. That guilt is because we went against what was right and good. It proves we have the terminal disease of spiritual cancer: sin. The person at the greatest risk of dying from physical or spiritual cancer is the one who denies that they have it. The results are devastating not only to them but to all those who are a part of their life.

Remember the combination of strategies needed for my wife's victorious battle over cancer? She had to listen to experts, do whatever was necessary and trust God through the entire ordeal. This same combination is how we are cured of spiritual cancer: Expert advice, proven treatment, total trust in God.

EXPERT ADVICE:
What Jesus says about sin

For this reason I told you that you'll die because of your sins. If you don't believe that I am the one, you'll die because of your sins.
John 8:24 GW

PROVEN TREATMENT:
What Jesus, the Savior, does to treat our spiritual cancer

Jesus was the only one ever born cancer-free. His spiritual DNA wasn't infected with this terminal illness, yet He chose to place all of our deadly sin in a syringe and inject Himself, paying the ultimate price on the cross. Out of deep compassion and perfect love, His death saved our lives.

> *He carried our sins in His own body when He died on a cross. In doing this, we may be dead to sin and alive to all that is right and good.*
> I Peter 2:24 GW

TOTAL TRUST:
What Jesus prescribes as the Key to Life

This treatment, however, will never work unless it is applied with total trust in Jesus—the only one who can cure.

> *Jesus said . . . "I am the one who brings people back to life, and I am life itself. Those who believe in me will live even if they die. Everyone who lives and believes in me will never die."*
> John 11:25–26 GW

We see in the Bible that religious people were always badgering Jesus. They believed the lie that the way to God was through doing good works or deeds. They asked Jesus what God wanted them to DO to be made right with Him. His answer may surprise you:

> *Jesus told them, "This is the only work God wants from you: Believe in the one he has sent."*
> John 6:29 NLT

The only thing God wants from us is total trust. Not works or deeds to earn His acceptance. Jesus has already DONE it all, for us.

If you're in awe of the love and kindness of God as you read this, that's normal. The Bible has a word to describe this lavishing of love on all who would trust Jesus: grace.

This is a word you will read many times in the New Testament of the Bible. It means, _receiving what I don't deserve_. Grace is God's love, presence, forgiveness and life. It's Jesus initiating our rescue. It's Jesus loving us when we had no love or interest in Him.

> *But God put his love on the line for us by offering his Son in sacrificial death while we were of no use whatever to him.*
> Romans 5:8 MSG

As a new follower of Jesus, I learned a little acrostic which helps me see *grace* in understandable, simple terms. It may help you as well.

GRACE is:
God's **R**iches **A**t **C**hrist's **E**xpense

We can receive peace, forgiveness and life (God's Riches) because Jesus died for us (Christ's Expense). The result of taking God's treatment is new life and transformation into a new creation, a creation without spiritual cancer.

We now live as God's free, loved, forgiven and cleansed children.

Why would Jesus do all of this? He did it for love, in order to restore us to God's original design of an unhindered relationship with Him and each other. This new life is summed up beautifully by the Apostle Paul in the following verse. It's a life where you and I are no longer at the center:

> *And He died for all, that those who live should no longer live for themselves but for Him who died for them and was raised again.*
> II Corinthians 5:15 NIV

As God's new creation, there is a shift that happens in you. You step into a life forgiven and free of living for yourself.

But how? That's what I would ask. They may have been able to live for Jesus in the first century because He was there with them, showing them, talking to them, encouraging them and doing miraculous things like feeding over 5,000 people in one meal (Matthew 14:13–21).

But how am I to follow Jesus' words and ways without Him around?

The simple answer is: by faith.

The full answer is: with His presence and help.

3. JESUS PROMISES THE SPIRIT: GOD LIVING IN US AND THROUGH US

When Jesus was baptized in the Jordan River, the voice of God the Father spoke from heaven saying, "You are my Son, whom I love; with you I am well pleased (Matthew 3:13–17)." But something else happened as well. The Spirit of God descended on Jesus in the form of a dove. The Spirit then led Jesus through the remainder of His earthly life and ministry. And He actually *raised Him from the grave* (Romans 8:11).

Jesus' promise and plan for our life, as His new creations, are what He modeled in His own life lived among us. When we put our full trust in Jesus, the same Spirit who descended on Him will dwell within us, affirming that we belong to God and showing us how to live for Him.

Wait a minute! Am I saying that in addition to God's forgiveness and total cure from spiritual cancer, in addition to a real and personal relationship with Him, in addition to God's love letter, the Bible, in addition to helping me know Him and follow Him,

He's also going to dwell within me by His Spirit and guide me as I learn to live as His new creation?

Yes! That's exactly what I'm saying.

Take a look at this passage and marvel at what Jesus said to His followers, and to us, before He returned to heaven:

> *"I will not leave you orphaned. I'm coming back. In just a little while the world will no longer see me, but you're going to see me because I am alive and you're about to come alive. At that moment you will know absolutely that I'm in my Father, and you're in me, and I'm in you. . .*
>
> *I'm telling you these things while I'm still living with you. The Friend, the Holy Spirit whom the Father will send at my request, will make everything plain to you. He will remind you of all the things I have told you. I'm leaving you well and whole. That's my parting gift to you. Peace."*
>
> John 14:18–20; 25–27 MSG

Living as a follower of Jesus does not equal being forgiven by God and now trying to keep your spiritual nose clean until you die. You can't anyway, no matter how hard you try. That would be going backward, not forward: back to a life of striving for "good enough."

Or, in a word: religion.

Instead, life as a **new creation** of God, a follower of Jesus, is lived *with* and *by* the power of God's Spirit, Who, in a manner of speaking, is Jesus living with us. (Remember the three-in-one Trinity?) Or, as you may have heard some say, "Jesus living in my heart."

> *God's Spirit is how Jesus can live*
> *in all of His followers at the same time.*

> *You can tell for sure that you are now fully adopted*
> *as his own children because God sent the Spirit of his*
> *Son into our lives crying out, "Papa! Father!" Doesn't*
> *that privilege of intimate conversation with God*
> *make it plain that you are not a slave, but a child?*
> Galatians 4:6–7 MSG

I know this is a lot to take in, and you may feel as though you've been drinking from a fire hose. Can I encourage you not to see this book as something to get through as fast as you can but, instead, to journey through it slowly, thoughtfully and prayerfully? In addition to underlining things, I often write my thoughts or questions in the margins of books I am reading. You might want to try recording your thoughts in the section set aside for *Living What We're Learning*. It's also very helpful to ask the Holy Spirit (talk to Him as you would to me if we were sitting together) to help you understand all that's happening inside you and all He wants to teach you. He's a good and patient teacher.

LIVING WHAT YOU'RE LEARNING

You've been learning some mind-boggling things, I know. Things like *spiritual cancer* and that Jesus stands out among all the world's religious deities and leaders as:

- God choosing to be with us
- God choosing to die for us
- God sending His Spirit to live in us.

This is a good place to breathe deeply and to thank God for loving you so much.

I've found it a good exercise to say out loud from time to time:

I am loved by God.

Can I invite you to say or write it, not once, but four or five times in a row? I encourage you to choose to believe this whether you feel it or not. When you do, you are affirming the most powerful reality in all of creation: God loves you!

Try it. I'll wait.

PRAYER

Holy Spirit, speak to each person reading these words so that they may begin to know the love of God in its fullness. Amen

CHAPTER 2
MAKING SURE YOU'RE HIS NEW CREATION

You might read the heading of this chapter and find yourself saying, "I thought I was sure. That's why I'm reading this book." But, after helping many people make the decision to become a follower of Jesus, I've discovered that it's important to make absolutely sure before we go any further. You see, in the Bible, most of the people who hung around Jesus, the multitudes, wanted what He had to give. But few wanted to follow Him. They gladly received His healing and greedily ate the bread and fish He miraculously gave them, but most of them were not willing to stop living for themselves and to start living for Him.

I'm going to say a couple of things that may bump you or, at the very least, challenge your thinking, either because you've been taught something different or because you've only seen a portion of the plan Jesus has for your life as His **brand new creation.** Are you ready? Here goes . . .

Jesus doesn't want your sins; He wants your life.

Remember God's original design? Unhindered relationship with Him and each other without the toxic effects of spiritual cancer.

Remember God's solution? Jesus coming to live _with us,_ love us in our messed up condition and provide forgiveness and a new life through faith in His perfect sacrifice on the cross and victorious resurrection from the dead.

Remember God's new design? (Don't be frustrated if you don't because I haven't really shared it yet.) His new design is the fulfillment of His original design: unhindered relationship with Him and with each other. For this new design to be experienced and lived, we have to decide to no longer be in control of things. In other words, we must choose to let God **be** God over everything in our lives, from now on.

The reason this is a new thought for many is because we can be so concerned about being forgiven and going to heaven that we often lose the whole point. Following Jesus is not primarily about going to heaven when we die, but about following Jesus all our lives.

Let's look at what Jesus said to the people as they followed Him around, gobbling-up whatever they could get from Him:

Then, calling the crowd to join his disciples, he [Jesus] said, "If any of you wants to be my follower, you must turn from your selfish ways, take up your cross, and follow me. If you try to hang on to your life, you will lose it. But if you give up your life for my sake and for the sake of the Good News, you will save it."

Mark 8:34–35 NLT

Intense! Is it any wonder that, when Jesus said things like this, the crowds thinned down? Let me explain this in a way I think you'll appreciate.

Do you own keys? I realize we live in an age where carrying physical keys is becoming less common. However, most of us still have them, use them and need them. Some have fobs, pass cards, and all of us have passwords giving us access to our online activities. Let's pretend our physical set of keys represent all of these variations. As a matter of fact, if you have your keys nearby, it actually would help to get them out at this point and set them in front of you. I know, I know, you just got comfortable in your favorite chair and are tempted to say, "Really? You want me to get my keys while I read this?" Yes, would you, please? I think you'll be glad you did.

Okay, got 'em out? Good.

Have you ever thought about your keys? They represent a lot of things, things like:

ownership
access
responsibility
privilege
security
provision
control

A key gets you in your house. A key starts your car. A key, or password, gives you access to your checking and savings accounts, as well as to your investments. A key lets you instantly buy far too much on Amazon. A key lets you, and no one else, use your smartphone or laptop. Keys lock things down and open things up.

We could even say they are "key" to our lives.

Here's where I want you to use your imagination. Think of the keys sitting in front of you as a representation of your life. They can represent your freedom (the car key); your family (your house key); your security now and in the future (the password to your accounts); your entertainment (password to your phone or computer); your intimate life (key to your bedroom) and on and on. Can you imagine how deep the impact on your life would be if one of these keys permanently vanished?

OWNERSHIP

ACCESS

CONTROL

SECURITY

RESPONSIBILITY

PRIVILEGE

PROVISION

Here's where it gets interesting. What binds all of your keys together? A key ring. And even _that_ says something about you. For me, a Mini Cooper ring with a Cooper icon corrals all of my keys. For our purpose, let's say that this little metal circle represents consolidated control of our lives. Lose the key ring, lose everything.

We trudge through life, keys jangling in our pockets at every step. Then Jesus comes along. We hear about Him from a friend or family member. Maybe we heard that He forgives. Something we didn't think was possible. Or we're drawn to Him because someone we love has died, and we know He talks about life after death.

Jesus then invites us to become His followers but first asks if He can have all of our keys. If your keys are there in front of you, would you play-act with me? Take them by the ring and hold them out, as if you were giving them to Jesus.

But! When Jesus takes ahold of the keys, very few people let go of the ring that keeps the keys all together.

I know this is a book, but would you humor me and act it out?

Hold the key ring with one of your hands and pull at the keys with your other.

Do you see it? A mini tug-of-war going on while you're reading.

Most people who hung around Jesus wanted what He had to give: healing, forgiveness, food, heaven. They didn't want Him for who He is. And Jesus is _God_ Himself. Jesus is the only one who knows what's best for our lives and can provide it. He is the one we must give the keys and the key ring to in order to be freed from the spiritual cancer that comes from controlling our own lives.

Remember what Jesus told the crowds and His followers in the passage we read? In light of our discussion on keys, you'll notice my paraphrase in the areas with brackets:

> _Then, calling the crowd to join his disciples, he [Jesus] said, "If any of you wants to be my follower [have a relationship with me], you must give up your own way [choose to put God first], take up your cross [a choice to stop living for self], and follow me [live out my words and ways]. If you try to hang on to your life [control it and live for yourself], you will lose it [never experience my love, forgiveness, peace and future]. But if you give up your life for my sake [hand me the keys and the ring] and for the sake of the Good News, you will save it [be healed and cleansed of spiritual cancer and become the person I've always meant for you to be]."_
> Mark 8:34–35 NLT [paraphrase added]

When you hand Jesus your keys, yet hang on to the key ring, you keep Him from becoming all He is in you and all He wants you to become. When you and I maintain control, in any area, we are continuing to act as "God" in our lives. And, according to Jesus, this will eventually result in a total loss of everything.

Now, this is where it gets good. Take your keys, hold them up, and ask this question: "Do I want Jesus to not only heal my spiritual cancer, but also to have my life to such an extent that He has the final say in every area?"

Don't be in a hurry to answer. Jesus told people to count the cost of following Him (Luke 14:25–34).

As you hold the keys in your hand, whose keys are they? They're yours, of course. Now, place them in your other hand (representing giving them to Jesus), and, this time, let them go and say, *"Jesus, every key and the ring are yours. I take my hands off completely."*

Now, as the hand representing Jesus' hand holds them, whose are they? They are now His, completely His. Did you see that? One moment they were yours, and, as a result of a simple, but very weighty decision, you gave them to Him.

Let me ask one more time. When you place them in the hand of Jesus, whose keys do they become? That's right: His.

Now, watch; He does the most stunning thing. The moment we place the keys fully in His hand, He puts them right back into ours.

Continuing our illustration, place the keys from your "Jesus" hand back into your other hand. Boom! I bet you closed your fingers around them a little when you got them back. It happens about every time. We're so used to gripping things in our lives that our fingers immediately clutch so we won't drop them.

Jesus peels back our fingers, opens our open palm, and says, "Whose keys are these now?"

The right answer?

"Jesus, these are Your keys from now on!"

Jesus becomes the owner, the one with the final say. The Bible uses the word Lord for the One with supreme authority over our lives. We now shift from being the _owner_ to being the _caretaker_ of our lives. A caretaker cares for something someone else owns.

As caretakers, we have a responsibility to care for His keys, and we have the privilege of using, living in, enjoying all the things the keys represent. This is what giving up ownership of our lives to Jesus looks like.

"But," you may ask, "if my hand is supposed to remain open, how do I keep from dropping the keys in the rough and tumble of life?" That's when Jesus wraps His strong, nail-scarred hand over yours and says, "This way: just hold on to me as I hold on to you."

Following Jesus is allowing Him to cleanse us, once and for all, and giving Him total ownership over all areas of our life (keys and ring).

Why take so much space to unpack this key illustration? Because I've found that many people either don't understand this foundation of becoming a follower of Jesus, or just want His forgiveness and not His ownership. **The life Jesus promises never works until we have both.**

Can I ask you a very important question?

Have you given up all of your keys?

I'm not asking if you have ever sought God for forgiveness of your sins or asked for help through a tough time. I'm not asking if you want to go to heaven.

Have you ever considered the claim that Jesus is God Himself, come to Earth, so that you may know Him personally by giving control of your life to Him once and for all?

If you have, this book is in celebration of what you've already decided. He's already filled you with peace and a new sense of purpose.

LIVING WHAT YOU'RE LEARNING

The most important purpose of this book is to help you be sure you're His and that He has every part of your life.

When I share these things people often say, "Well, when I was thirteen, I asked Jesus to forgive me and come into my heart, so I'm in, right?" I can't say if a person is "in" or not, but I can ask if you've ever given Jesus not only your sin, but also absolute control of your life. I can also ask if your life changed once you began to live His way and not your own.

Many hesitate at this point and often say they want to but are afraid they will take their lives back or blow it somehow. _Well, of course they will_. We are still broken people after all. Jesus knows this; we all fail as we follow Him. Remember, being a new creation is not about living a perfect life, it's about trusting and following Jesus. And when we give Him everything, His Spirit will teach us to take control of our lives less and less.

If you have never handed your life over to Jesus, would you like to right now? If you need more time to think about it and to consider all the keys involved, I applaud you. Choosing to be a follower of Jesus is the most important decision we'll ever make. It must never be decided lightly.

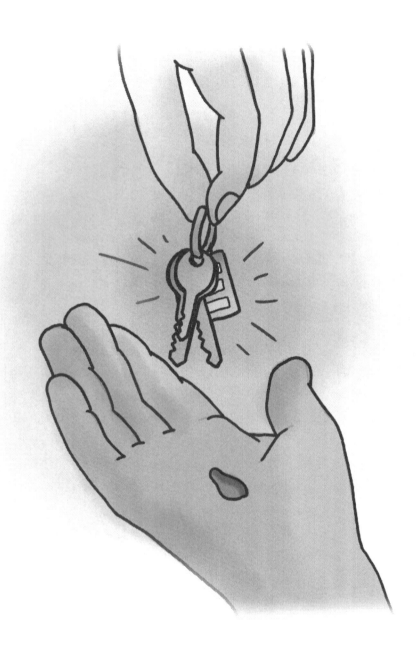

If you're ready, I want to ask you to pray a prayer of releasing your spiritual cancer <u>and</u> control to Him. You can pray it in your heart, but I've found that saying it out loud, for some reason, has great power. Please, look the prayer over before you pray it. Forget about where you are right now and realize that it's just you and God. Let's pray:

PRAYER

Dear God, thank you for sending your Son, Jesus, so that I could be forgiven and know You; I want to confess all the spiritual cancer in my life which the Bible calls sin. I have blown it, hurt You and hurt others time and time again. I know I can't make up for all of the things I've done. I come asking for your forgiveness and mercy because of what Jesus did by dying on the cross for me. I'm coming clean with you. I need your total cleansing. I believe you alone can free me from my sin, and I receive your forgiveness and freedom by faith right now!

I not only release my sin to you, but I also give you everything: all the keys, the key ring and the right to have the final say in my life. I give you the control. I give up. I'm yours from now on. Thank you for taking my sin away. And thank you for taking the life I've given you and placing it back in my hands, where I'm no longer to be the owner but a follower. I will follow where you lead me and do what you tell me. Thank you, Jesus. I declare you to be the Lord of my life, the leader over everything, the One I pledge my full allegiance to. Amen, so be it from now on!

Yes! You did it! You've handed all of who you are—past, present and future—over to God! God says you are now His, and He is now yours. Your past is completely forgiven and gone. You are actually, in this instant, a new creation! God's new creation. His beloved daughter or son from now on!

> *Whoever is a believer in Christ is a new creation. The old way of living has disappeared. A new way of living has come into existence.*
> II Corinthians 5:17 GW

His Spirit has just entered your spirit for the very first time to take up permanent residence in you! He wants you to experience from now on the overwhelming confidence that comes with knowing you belong to Jesus.

> *This is what God told us: God has given us eternal life, and this life is in his Son. Whoever has the Son has life, but whoever does not have the Son of God does not have life.*
> I John 5:11–12 ERV

This is a great place to pause and let the love of God fill you right where you are.

You <u>are</u> loved by God and are now forgiven and at peace with Him.

In the space below, why don't you record the date and time you made this commitment, whether it was prior to picking up this book or right this moment. In the shifting challenges of life, it will serve as a type of pillar for you to return to throughout your journey as a follower of Jesus. It will also serve as the marker of your spiritual birthday. The day you became a new creation.

I, _____

(your name)

have decided to follow Jesus and to yield
all of the keys of my life to Him.
I put my faith in Jesus' shed blood for my total forgiveness
and put my life under His loving leadership (Lordship) on

_____.

(date)

I record this to remind myself of my pledge
of total allegiance to Jesus as the only way to life
and to His Kingdom (ways).

Signed with all my love,

_____

(your signature)

54

One of the most powerful things you can do now is to tell someone! You don't have to describe what happened perfectly but one of the most ancient practices of all followers of Jesus has been to "go public" with their commitment to follow Him.

I'm not talking about a soap box or global post on Twitter or anything. I'm talking about telling someone you know and who knows and respects you. If no one comes to mind and you are a part of a church, find your pastor and tell them. Just watch how excited they get for you.

Something happens when you share with someone. For real. That's why the Bible tells us to do so. I even invite you to let me know as well. I'd love to celebrate with you.

You can email me at
seniorleadership@discoverlifegate.com

YOUR GROWTH

CHAPTER 3
STAY CONNECTED WITH JESUS

For those who don't know me, I'm married and happy. I add the "and happy" part because some people believe that when you get married, the drudgery begins. Nothing could be further from the truth. But, it didn't necessarily start easy. No matter how much a person knows about marriage, they discover how ignorant they are once they actually say, "I do." The giant magnifying glass of marriage soon hovers over them and reveals how totally addicted to _self_ we all tend to be. Then children come along and ratchet up the magnification to excruciating levels of scrutiny. In both cases, _everything_ changes. I share these examples because they illustrate two of life's most serious and fulfilling relationships.

Just as when you marry or have children, when you decide to follow Jesus, _everything_ changes because you have decided to no longer view life as all about you. This new reality is only possible by God's power, a power found as you cultivate and strengthen your relationship with Him.

There are many, but I want to lay out for you four practices which I have found helpful in growing in my relationship with Jesus. I believe they will help you as well.

> **The 4 practices are:**
> - **Stay Connected** with Jesus
> - **Start Learning** about Jesus
> - **Share Life** in Your New Community
> - **Show and Tell**

Relationship is about a commitment to stay connected. Even though we were guilty and our lives focused on ourselves, God invited us to have a relationship and to become eternally connected with Jesus. Jesus actually calls us His friends (John 15:15)! And God our Father calls us His children (I John 3:1)! This unhindered relationship with God is what life is all about. It's a friendship that gets better and better every single day.

Here are three things you can do to stay connected with Jesus.

— PRAY —

I can't tell you how many times someone has said to me, "I don't know how to pray" or "I'm not comfortable with prayer!" I believe part of the reason we say this is because we don't understand what prayer is.

Prayer is talking with God (Jesus), listening to Jesus, and being with Jesus.

Prayer is NOT a religious speech you've prepared to impress God, or others, or even yourself. It is simply living life with God at the center. It's when we talk with God, Jesus or the Spirit of God out loud or in our hearts. If you know how to think or talk, you already know how to pray.

Another way to describe prayer is staying in touch. Friendships thrive on _staying in touch_. You and I are in touch constantly via social media. God is asking us to put Him in the most-important-person category of your daily connections, at the very top of your favorites list.

Remember, prayer is also listening to God. He speaks through impressions we feel in our hearts, through His living Word (the Bible), through circumstances and through other people. What He says to us is always loving. He never condemns us (though He may correct us) and never goes against what He's said in the Bible.

My wife, Kris, and I listen to God all the time. One of our favorite practices is listening to God in restaurants, airplanes, stores, any place public. We have found that when we take the time to listen, God takes that opportunity to speak to us through an impression, a whisper or through Kris and I coming up with the same thought "out of the blue." We have prayed for so many waiters and waitresses over the years that when we are out, one of us will inevitably say, "I think God is wanting us to give them more than a tip." And the other will say, "What?! I was thinking the same thing!"

Then things get fun.

Kris will say, "How much?"

"How much do you think?" I'll respond.

"You tell me first."

We'll volley back and forth for a minute or two. Then one of us will say a number, "$100!"

And, seemingly without fail, the other will say, "I was thinking the exact same thing!"

In those moments, we believe God is speaking to us at the same time and that it's confirmed by us hearing the same amount to give. The other confirmation is the shock we see on our server's face, with tears tumbling out of their eyes. Often, we never find out why God asks us to be generous in those situations. But He knows why.

Prayer is not rocket science. It's trusting God enough to talk with Him and listen to Him.

Still not convinced? Maybe this will help. Did you know God hears weak prayers? He does. Read what the Bible says about you and me:

> *If we don't know how or what to pray, it doesn't*
> *matter. He does our praying in and for us . . .*
> Romans 8:26 MSG

This verse tells us God's Spirit will teach us, will inspire prayer in us and will even pray (talk to God) for us!

And the Holy Spirit helps us in our weakness. For example, we don't know what God wants us to pray for. But the Holy Spirit prays for us with groanings that cannot be expressed in words. And the Father who knows all hearts knows what the Spirit is saying, for the Spirit pleads for us believers in harmony with God's own will.

Romans 8:26–27 NLT

God is more interested in you staying connected with Him than He is in you saying and praying all the right things. I talk to God all day long. I start my day by saying or thinking, "Good morning, Jesus! I love you!" I end my day with something like, "Thank you, My God, for being so present, so faithful through this day. Please watch over my family, our church, the desperately needy in my city and over me this night."

LIVING WHAT YOU'RE LEARNING

Why not apply what you're learning about prayer? I often write to God as I would write a letter. This is a form of prayer. Take a few minutes and express your gratitude to God on the lines provided, listen for His whisper (which often comes as passing thoughts you wouldn't normally think) and then ask Him for something you or someone else needs. I'm not giving you too many lines because I mean for this to be brief.

MY PRAYER:

– TRUST –

Faith is the ability to believe something, the ability to trust something or someone without being able to see with our eyes. We exercise faith every day without realizing it.

- We turn on our smartphones with a push of our finger, believing it will come on again. Without understanding all the intricacies of how it functions, we just believe it will.

- We start our cars, turn on the lights of our homes, open up the faucet for fresh water, all by faith. The more we do these things, believe in processes we can't see or understand, the more confident we become.

- Driving down the street, we have faith that the car coming from the other direction won't swerve and hit us.

All relationships involve faith. Another way to describe faith is "trust." *Merriam-Webster Online Dictionary* defines trust this way:

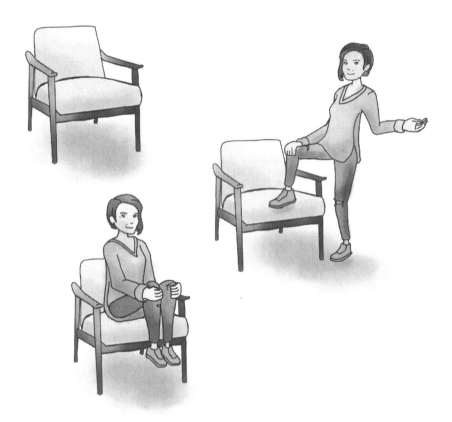

Trust assured reliance on the character, ability, strength, or truth of someone

Who do you trust? I mean really trust? If you've lived life for very long, you've most likely been hurt by other people. The hurts we feel most deeply are from those we trusted most. For example, if you were once married, you entrusted yourself to your spouse. But, if your marriage has broken up, you may not be sure if you can ever trust enough to be married again. We face the "what ifs" of a broken marriage or friendship or business partnership.

What if the same thing happens again? What if I let my guard down, and, this time, I get hurt even worse than the last time? What if I have to be alone the rest of my life because of my fear?

Your "truster" could have been damaged. That vulnerable, transparent part of you God created so we could bond and build enduring marriages and friendships has been broken.

I will never forget this true story, told by a man who walked with a permanent limp. When I asked about the limp, the man described, in this heartbreaking story, how it was the result of broken trust.

When this man was a boy, he lived in fear of his very demanding and cruel father. He loved his dad very much but found it so hard to trust him because of his harsh comments and treatment.

One day, when he was four years old and living on the farm where he grew up, he was in the hay barn with his dad who was stacking hay, high up into the barn.

His dad was rarely, if ever, playful, but, on this day, he said, "Hey, Son, climb up on the hay and jump down; I'll catch you!"

The man remembers responding, "I don't know, Daddy; I'm afraid; it's so high."

Inside, he recounts that it was more than the height; it was wondering why his demanding dad was suddenly playful.

"It'll be like flying! I'll be right here and catch you!" said his dad.

But, he didn't.

The boy finally trusted his dad and was attracted to his outstretched arms and big smile and said, "Okay, Daddy, here I come! Catch me!"

And he jumped.

At the last second, his dad quickly moved out of the way and let his son fall on the hard, concrete barn floor. And the boy was hurt.

Through his sobs, he heard his dad's raised voice laughing

and shouting, "You see, Stupid? That'll teach you to _ever_ trust a family member!"

Although the boy's parents never took him to the hospital (he could still walk), he was permanently damaged.

Later, as an adult, because of the lifetime of pain he endured, the man had the damage checked. The x-ray revealed the place where the boy had broken his lower back that day in the barn and how it had healed out of alignment.

Is it any wonder this man had a difficult time trusting other men, authority figures or God? But that wasn't the only misalignment in his life. He struggled with trust in every relationship in his life. He had an especially hard time trusting God.

But, he eventually did, and here's how.

He encountered people in his life who had become **brand new** and had entrusted their lives to Jesus. It wasn't right away though. He watched their lives, became their casual friends and then experienced their kindness and consistent friendship and love. They stuck around when times were rough. They thought more of him than they did of themselves. They proved their trustworthiness.

You see, trust is an easy thing to lose, but it's very difficult to earn back.

God knows all of this. He knows that releasing control of your life and entrusting yourself to Him is, for some, the hardest, scariest thing they will ever do.

I'm so grateful He proved His trustworthiness by loving you so much that He didn't just talk about it. To show us His love, He sent Jesus to live _with us_ on this Earth filled with broken relationships and damaged trust. He also sent Him to die for us and forever prove how much He loves us.

Jesus' call to follow Him is a call to trust Him. It involves believing in who He is and what He has done and said. It involves faith.

The faith/trust you've exercised by believing Jesus died on a cross, for you, and rose from the grave is what I call "saving" faith because it resulted in you being saved or rescued from the consequences of your soul cancer as well as from its daily influence. It has resulted in you being forgiven and becoming a **brand new** creation. You're experiencing a new level of peace, joy and hope as you never have before.

Faith pleases God. Faith shows you trust God and are willing to let all of the keys of your life rest in His hands and to receive fully His love, His care and His plans.

The way to live as God's new creation is to trust Jesus, not only for your salvation but for your entire life. Jesus wants to become your daily, moment-by-moment Savior and Lord and not just someone you think about at church once a week. Here's what the Bible says about His trustworthiness:

> *God has said, "I will never fail you. I will never abandon you."*
> Hebrews 13:5 NLT

That's God's way of saying, "I'm never going to fool you, harm you or drop you."

When you decide to trust God moment-by-moment, you start to experience His presence and guidance in ways you could never imagine. How? The following Scripture from Proverbs captures, in simple terms, how we are to trust God and expect supernatural results:

> *Trust God from the bottom of your heart; Don't try to figure out everything on your own. Listen for God's voice in everything you do, everywhere you go; He's the one who will keep you on track.*
> Proverbs 3:5–6 MSG

Are there situations in your life that trouble you? Do they feel too big for you to handle or too complex for you to figure out? Jesus' invitation is that before you do anything in life, trust Him and tell Him so. Realize He has wisdom and direction beyond your own understanding. Talk with God, trust

God, hand things to God, and He will make a way in your life where there may seem to be no way at all. He's asking you to depend on Him, to walk hand in hand with Him and to trust Him alone.

Has your "truster" ever been damaged by people you've known or loved? Does this section make you feel sick to your stomach because you don't want to be hurt again? I totally get where you're coming from. I've been hurt as well. Our adversary, the Devil, likes to remind us of our wounds so we'll put trust in ourselves, which is just a variation of sin, or spiritual cancer.

There was a time in my life when I was betrayed by a very close, lifelong friend. My world was rocked. I was in a fog of disbelief for months until I realized that this really _did_ happen. (I'm sure some of you reading this can relate or you may have experienced another one of life's ultimate betrayals, divorce.) I began to make a vow to myself that went like this: I will never trust another person in my life.

The reason for such a vow is understandable. This was the best way to avoid getting hurt again. But God had other plans. According to Proverbs 3:5–6, I was _figuring things out on my own_ and not depending on Him. Thankfully, He whispered to my heart, "I have not said to stop trusting." _What? Who are you to say I have to trust again?_

Then I remembered who owns the keys to my life.

God used a well-known Christian author to help me understand more fully what He was telling me:

> *"To love at all is to be vulnerable. Love anything and your heart will be wrung and possibly broken. If you want to make sure of keeping it intact you must give it to no one, not even an animal. Wrap it carefully round with hobbies and little luxuries; avoid all entanglements. Lock it up safe in the casket or coffin of your selfishness. But in that casket, safe, dark, motionless, airless, it will change. It will not be broken; it will become unbreakable, impenetrable, irredeemable. To love is to be vulnerable."*
> —C.S. Lewis, *The Four Loves*

"But, Lord," I asked, "How can I trust without being totally hurt all the time?" His answer was that I should give only portions of my trust to people and only to those in relationship with me and that I should entrust myself completely only to Him.

In spite of the wounds you've experienced in life, God is still asking you to trust Him, put your full weight on Him and commit to receiving His care. Jesus even describes His Spirit—who now lives in you—as the "Comforter."

But when the Father sends the Comforter . . . the Holy Spirit—He will teach you much, as well as remind you of everything I myself have told you.
John 14:26 TLB

One of the most beautiful descriptions of our God is found in Psalm 23. I know you've probably heard this Psalm somewhere. But you may have never seen it as God promising to care for all who put their trust in Him.

Take a moment and read this Psalm slowly. In it, God is described as a loving shepherd, and we are His sheep. As I mentioned earlier, reading God's love letter, the Bible, out loud can be a very powerful experience. If you are in a coffee shop or in the library, you can even whisper it. Here goes . . .

The Lord is my best friend and my shepherd.
I always have more than enough.

He offers a resting place for me in His
luxurious love. His tracks take me to an
oasis of peace, the quiet brook of bliss.

That's where He restores and revives my life.
He opens before me pathways to God's
pleasure and leads me along in His
footsteps of righteousness so that
I can bring honor to His name.

Lord, even when your path takes me through
*   the valley of the deepest darkness,*
*   fear will never conquer me, for you*
*   already have! You remain close to me*
*   and lead me through it all the way.*
*   Your authority is my strength and*
*   my peace. The comfort of your love*
*   takes away my fear. I'll never be*
*   lonely, for you are near.*

You become my delicious feast even when my
*   enemies dare to fight. You anoint me*
*   with the fragrance of your Holy Spirit;*
*   you give me all I can drink of you until*
*   my heart overflows. So why would I fear*
*   the future?*

For your goodness and love pursue me all
*   the days of my life. Then afterward,*
*   when my life is through, I'll return*
*   to your glorious presence to be*
*   forever with you!*

Psalm 23:1–6, *The Passion Version*

Such a loving and faithful God, He can be trusted. He loves you. He's faithful to go with you and even to heal the areas where your heart has been cut, bruised or broken.

LIVING WHAT YOU'RE LEARNING

Are you ready to start? In the space below, tell God about the greatest obstacle you face in trusting Him. Don't be afraid to be honest; He can take it. After that, write down three areas where you want to trust God fully. I know this may feel painful to some but, like physical therapy after surgery, you can do this, and it will help your move more freely in trust.

My greatest obstacle to trusting God is:

_____

_____

_____

I will trust God completely in the following areas/needs of my life:

1. _____

2. _____

3. _____

PRAYER

Lord Jesus, thank You for the willingness of Your follower who is reading my words, to trust You. I pray You would fill their hearts with the confidence to know You are right there with them, and that You will show Yourself faithful in all the areas they are entrusting to You. I pray for their hearts to experience peace and any healing they may need, in Your mighty name!

— OBEY —

Have you ever noticed how a two-year-old's favorite word is not "please" or "thank you?"

It's "NO!"

I added the exclamation point because little children don't say it quietly. Instead, it bursts out of their mouths:

"NO!"

We live in a broken world, and one of the earliest expressions of our brokenness is the bent toward ourselves. We want our way, when we want it, the way we want it. And so the conflict begins. We want to get close to a hot stove, but our mother tells us not to touch it. We say, "NO!" and reach out to touch it anyway. We want to run in the street, but our dad tells us to stay on the sidewalk. We say, "NO!" and hop off the curb anyway.

One of the most important things our parents teach us is how to obey. Ideally, they want us to obey them so that we might experience what's best for us and be protected from those things that could cause harm.

Obedience helps us experience what's best for us and protects us from those things that could cause harm.

This is a difficult process because the drive to have our own way is very strong. Some call it our fallen nature or our flesh.

Please, don't get me wrong. We want kids to explore and be increasingly independent of mom and dad, up to the point of leaving home and starting out on their own. But there are boundaries in life, rules we must follow. Gravity is a law we must respect or be hurt by. Following the direction of our parents, teachers and public safety individuals is essential to having a fruitful life lived in harmony with others.

Obedience is one of the first lessons we must learn in life and one of the hardest lessons to learn well.

Why the big explanation about little kids, rules, etc.? Because following Jesus involves obedience. Would you pause a moment and let those words sink in? There is a tendency in all of us to pursue God for what *He* can do for *us*—and He wants to do many, many things. However, God, the Creator of all things, the One who gave His only Son to suffer and die for you and me, wants to teach us to live a life that doesn't focus on ourselves, but on Him and others.

There are three big reasons why He calls us to a life of loving obedience. First, because He is God and deserves our obedience. Second, because everything He calls us to do is for our benefit and the benefit of others. Finally, because He wants to protect us from things that could harm us and from the one (Satan) who is always trying to deceive you and me into doing things our own way, not God's way. You may remember that's what we called "spiritual cancer" in a previous chapter.

You may have heard of the best-selling book entitled *The Purpose Driven Life* written by Rick Warren. It's a tremendous book about living for God and discovering the life of purpose He offers. The very first words, in the very first chapter, are vitally important to embrace if you are to experience life as God's new creation.

It's not about you.
—Rick Warren

Our lives as followers of Jesus begin with our decision to confess our self-focus (spiritual cancer), turn from a life lived for ourselves and then to choose to follow Jesus as the Lord/Leader of our lives. This means He has the final say. This means we choose to do whatever He leads us to do.

Learning to obey Jesus is a process, much like a child learning how to obey their parents. It involves success and failure. It's hardest for those who thought following Jesus was about what they could get _from_ Him, rather than who they can become _in_ Him, and what they can do <u>for</u> Him.

Here is a Scripture where Jesus confronts many people's tendencies to say they want to follow Him, but they keep on living for themselves.

Why are you so polite with me, always saying "Yes, sir," and "That's right, sir," but never doing a thing I tell you? These words I speak to you are not mere additions to your life, homeowner improvements to your standard of living. They are foundation words, words to build a life on.

Luke 6:46–47 MSG

No one has ever loved more or sacrificed more so that you could receive a forgiven, abundant, new life. And only one person can have the final say in this new life, and that is Jesus, our life-giver.

*If you love me, keep my commands. . . Anyone who loves me will **obey** my teaching. My Father will love them, and we will come to them and make our home with them. Anyone who does not love me will not **obey** my teaching.*

John 14:15, 23–24 NIV [emphasis added]

*I've loved you the way my Father has loved me. Make yourselves at home in my love. If you keep **my commands,** you'll remain intimately at home in my love. That's what I've done—kept my Father's commands and made myself at home in his love. I've told you these things for a purpose: that my joy might be your joy, and your joy wholly mature. This is **my command:** Love one another the way I loved you. This is the very best way to love. Put*

your life on the line for your friends. You are my
*friends when you **do the things I command you.***
John 15:9–14 MSG [emphasis added]

I realize a lot of these things may be **brand new** ideas to you. I encourage you to take moments to stop and think about what you're reading. And talk with God. Remember, I said this is a process. It's really the process of growing up, in Him.

In reading that last verse, you might have been thrown by the phrase, "keep my commands." In our B.C. (Before Christ) lives, we thought the only way to God was to keep His laws, to be as good as we can. But, earlier in this book, we learned that doing so is an insurmountable task. We can never be good enough. It's impossible.

Now that we've chosen Jesus, all of the commandments of God have been simplified to just two:

Jesus replied, "You must love the Lord your
God with all your heart, all your soul, and all
your mind. This is the first and greatest
commandment. A second is equally important:
Love your neighbor as yourself."
Matthew 22:37–39 NLT

Once we surrender our lives to the complete and loving leadership of Jesus, we now love Him and others <u>because</u> we want to live the life He desires us to live. Lots of people around the world are trying to obey a misconceived God because they fear judgment and punishment. That's not what should motivate you or me. We are motivated by love and a deep gratitude for what Jesus has done.

Obedience is not to be motivated by fear of punishment but by love and a deep gratitude for what Jesus has done.

When I was in graduate school studying for my Master's degree, I had a dog named Princess. She was half golden lab and half German shepherd. She looked like a golden shepherd. I used to take her to the gym where I'd lift weights. Princess wasn't allowed in but, because the weight room was on the ground

SHE | SHE
LOVES | OBEYS
ME | ME

level, I would leave her outside with a tennis ball to help keep her focused during my hour-long workout.

Princess loved to fetch. About every five minutes or so, I would go the gym window, reach my hand under her mouth and say, "Princess, drop it." She would drop the ball; then I'd throw it for her. She faithfully brought it back to me, every time, over and over and over, her body always shaking with excitement as she grinned at me (I think dogs can smile).

Often, someone in the weight room, who had no experience with Princess, would go over to toss the ball for her. They would put their hand out the window, but Princess wouldn't get close. Frustrated, they would say, "Princess, drop it!" She never would. This scenario was repeated over and over again in the five years I worked out at that particular gym. She never would obey anyone but me.

I have to admit her loyal obedience gave me a great sense of pride. Especially when I would go over to the window, after someone's failed attempt, reach out and say, "Princess, drop it, " and, of course, she would.

I mattered, and they didn't. *Ha!*

I had the say.

I was the master, and they weren't.

One day after being especially taken by her faithfulness to me, I returned home and found myself telling my wife, "She's such an amazing dog! She loves me. She obeys me!"

At that moment, I heard the quiet whisper of God's Spirit ask, "Did you hear the words you just said? They are very important to remember, Son. The way you love Jesus most is by faithfully obeying Him alone."

I have never forgotten that moment. Princess would listen to me above everything else. God wants us to listen to _Him_ above everything else. Princess was a one-man dog. I alone was her master. Jesus wants His followers to be obedient to one Master, and that is Him. Do you see it?

My obedience to God declares that
life is not about me but about Jesus and
what He thinks is best for me.

God is very kind to show us, slowly, all the ways we need to obey Him rather than all at once. He leads us just as we lead our children, from one step to the next. He's a good Father, patient, kind and loving. Even when we blow it, He keeps loving us and inviting us to try again. I love this about our great God! I've messed up so many times since I gave my life to Jesus, and He has never condemned me nor left me (Romans 8:1). And He will never condemn or leave you.

I remember a big step God asked me to take the first few months of following Him. I was trusting Him and had given over my life, well, all except for one thing I still held on to.

I was seriously dating a person who did not believe in the truth of God or want to believe that Jesus alone could make us into a new creation. I tried to convince myself that it was okay to have God and her at the same time. But God's Spirit whispered that she was not in His plan for my future. I'd argue with this voice and insisted I could love God fully and love her, too. I told Him I'd marry her and try very hard to daily draw her to Him. He told me that only He could draw her. He wanted me to let her go and follow Him alone.

Did you know God rarely tells us when He's testing us? He wanted to see if I was willing to forsake all others for Him and obey Him no matter what the cost. But, I was failing the test. For six long months, I continued to argue with God. Can you relate? Is there something in your life, deep inside your heart, that you know God is asking you to change? Are you trying to negotiate with Him? How's that working for ya? One way you'll know when you aren't obeying is that you will lack peace. It's like having spiritual heartburn.

Finally, one night I was out walking my dog and asking God to let her be the one for me. (Aren't you glad He doesn't answer prayers that are bad for us?) At that moment, I had the impression to look up into the starry sky, and in my mind's eye flashed two images. Some would call it a day dream; others would call it a vision from God.

On the left, I saw Jesus, hanging on the cross, blood dripping down from his pierced and torn body. On the right, I saw the girl I was still dating.

And then it happened. I heard the whisper of God in my heart say, "Choose now who you will live for." The vision was so real and the voice so clear that I fell on my knees in my driveway and began to weep. I begged God to forgive me for letting this girl become an idol in my life that I had been refusing to give up. I told Him I wanted to live for Him alone. (I know, looks weird doesn't it? A person drives by and sees this guy on his knees bawling in his driveway. But I didn't care. All I wanted was to love Jesus and follow Him!)

The next morning, I drove seven hours, in the snow, to where she lived in Pittsburgh. I told her in person that I had to break up with her and pled with her to surrender her life to Jesus alone. She told me she wasn't interested in my brand of religion, and I left broken-hearted but thankful for the courage to obey God's clear leading.

LIVING WHAT YOU'RE LEARNING

Are there any areas of your life, big or small, where God is wanting your obedience? Do you find yourself arguing with Him, or perhaps avoiding Him in an attempt to hide it (I hate to tell you this, but He knows everything; He's God!)? Are you afraid you'll lose something you can't live without or miss out on something by obeying?

God is using my words to ask you once again to choose His way. To obey pleases God, it shows Him you love Him.

This may be taking you off-guard because it brings to mind something you've either been hiding or holding on to tightly. Would you listen to God's kind whisper and take the step of obedience? You won't be sorry you did, and God will give you strength to continue loving and obeying Him. Be courageous and pray the following if you feel led to:

PRAYER

God, I thank you for being so loving and patient with me. I want to be a true follower of Jesus and show it by always obeying Him. Thank you for speaking to me about:

_____.

(an area in which He's calling you to obey)

I choose obedience to Jesus right now and commit to:

_____.

(what you believe He's calling you to do)

I trust You for the ability to follow through and thank You for Your love and leadership in my life. In the name of Jesus, my Master. Amen.

In this section on staying connected with Jesus, we've talked about the three important practices of a growing relationship with Him:

1. **Prayer** – talking to God and listening for His voice
2. **Trust** – inviting Jesus into every moment of every day as you put your faith in Him
3. **Obedience** – listening to the whisper of God's Spirit and courageously doing what He says.

I want to emphasize, once again, this is a process. Like any relationship, it takes time and experience. You may be tempted to ask, "Will I ever get this? Will I ever hear God's whisper?"

I've asked the same things over the years of following Jesus, and I can answer you confidently, _Yes! You will start to get this. A little bit at a time_. A big plus is that there are people all around you who are on the same journey. You aren't alone.

CHAPTER 4
START LEARNING ABOUT JESUS

I'm not a golfer. I've never had a real desire to golf. Okay, true confessions? Golfing has intimidated me. I've swung a club a few times, and it feels as though I'm trying to be some kind of contortionist. Nothing feels normal. I feel weird. But, some time ago, I was a part of my younger brother's wedding, and part of the pre-wedding bachelor party activities was to drive golf balls. We went to this place in Dallas that had two tiers of people hitting golf balls out into a field with huge targets on the ground, each the size of my back yard!

Do you think I was excited? I was like, "Oh, great! I get to hang around some guys I barely know and do something I don't even like!"

You'll never believe what happened. Ready for this? I LOVED IT! Well, not at first. When one of the guys, Jonathan, who was half my age, stepped up and offered to help, I learned what to do.

I actually hit the ball, and, frankly, hit the ball well, more than a couple of times! I'd actually like to do it again and maybe even play golf one day.

Don't get me wrong. I was very tempted to opt out of the event with the excuse of being "athletically challenged." But on the way to the range, I decided I would do it for my brother. I want to pause here. Something happens to us, _in us,_ and _through us_ any time we decide to do something that focuses on someone other than ourselves. God gives special ability when we shift our focus to others. Want to know the crazy thing that always thrills me? When I focus on others, I'm always more fulfilled than if I'd focused on myself. Go figure! But it's true, and, as a matter of fact, that's how God has designed us.

Okay, I can hear you asking, "So why all the golf talk?" It's to illustrate that, often, when we have an opportunity to learn something new, we can be intimidated hesitant, and even unwilling, depending on our past experiences.

Would you continue to let me be your _learning_ coach just as Jonathan was my golfing coach?

Three areas I want to help you learn about are:
- Knowing God, not just knowing about Him
- Studying God's Word, His love letter and manual for life
- Discovering God's ways, _His Kingdom Come_.

— KNOWING GOD —

We live in the most amazing time in history. Because of technology and the Internet, a person can find out all kinds of things about almost anyone. If we're interested in going out with someone, we wouldn't think of asking them without checking their social media pages first. We fall in love with TV shows because we that we know the characters. But, there's a huge difference between knowing *about* someone and *actually* knowing them.

The biggest difference is that knowing someone means that they know you, too. This is relationship.

As you're getting started in your walk with God, it is important for you to learn that God knows you and wants you to know Him.

Christianity is the only faith on Earth in which the Founder calls us to enter a real relationship that is personal, with Him!

Don't believe me? Watch this! Jesus actually defines eternal life not as a quantity of life (living forever) but as a quality of life (living in relationship with God). Let these amazing words Jesus prayed sink in:

> *And this is the real and eternal life: That they **know you,** the one and only true God, and Jesus Christ, whom you sent.*
>
> John 17:3 MSG [emphasis added]

That's why you'll find that, throughout the Bible, God's first concern is not serving Him, giving to Him or telling about Him; it's _knowing_ Him. Though many, many things try to distract us, following Jesus is about a real, growing, experiential relationship. He is so committed to us knowing Him that He promises to invest in this relationship continuously and invites us to do the same.

I love the story in the beginning part of the Bible (the Old Testament) where God is leading His people out of slavery in Egypt to the land He promised them. On the way, Moses has a concern about God sticking with them all the way. Notice God's amazing answer:

> The Lord replied, "My Presence will go with you, and I will give you rest." Then Moses said to him, "If your Presence does not go with us, do not send us up from here. How will anyone know that you are pleased with me and with your people unless you go with us? What else will distinguish me and your people from all the other people on the face of the Earth?" And the Lord said to Moses, "I will do the very thing you have asked, because I am pleased with you and I **know you** by name."
> Exodus 33:14–17 NIV [emphasis added]

Moses' question is a huge one! "How else will anyone know that you are pleased with me and your people unless you go with us?

What else will distinguish me and your people from all the other people [and religions] on the face of the Earth?"

The thing that sets apart followers of Jesus is that they know God by experience and that God knows them.

Here are a few other portions of the Bible concerning knowing God and experiencing His presence:

> This is what the LORD says: "Don't let the wise boast in their wisdom, or the powerful boast in their power, or the rich boast in their riches. But those who wish to boast should boast in this alone: that they **truly know me** and understand that I am the Lord who demonstrates unfailing love and who brings justice and righteousness to the earth, and that I delight in these things.
> Jeremiah 9:23–24 NLT [emphasis added]

> I'm an open book to you **[the writer says to God]**; even from a distance, you **know** what I'm thinking. You **know** when I leave and when I get back; I'm never out of your sight. You **know** everything I'm going to say before I start the first sentence. I look behind me and you're there, then up ahead and you're there, too— your reassuring presence, coming and going. This is too much, too wonderful— I can't take it all in!
> Psalm 139:1–6 MSG [emphasis added]

*[Jesus said to His disciples] And be sure of this: I
am **with you always,** even to the end of the age.*
Matthew 28:20 NLT [emphasis added]

God's greatest longing is for a relationship with you that is
personal and real. Try to always remember this.

Not everyone reading this has been married, but marriage
is a good example of what I'm talking about. The heart of
any marriage is love and commitment between two people.
Everything revolves around this, but life is full. We have jobs,
cars, emails, appointments, homes, babies; the list is endless. If
a couple isn't careful, all the tasks of life will pick away at what's
really important. They can start to feel distant and disconnected
even though they live in the same house. Successful relationships
demand commitment and quality time together.

In all your learning as a follower of Jesus, remember this: It's
first about a relationship with God, where you know Him by
experience, and He knows you. This is what sets Jesus' offer of
life apart from all other religious offers in the world.

At Lifegate Church in Omaha, Nebraska, where I pastor, we
call this *thirsting first for God*. Let me end this section with a
description of King David. You may have heard of him before
in the well-known song Hallelujah by Leonard Cohen. He was
the king over Israel and pleased God so much that He called
David, "a man after My own heart." Do you know what made

David such a man? His *thirst first,* to know God and to live in His presence!

Although King David had a grueling schedule, running from his enemies and then eventually leading God's people for 40 years, he revealed the real love and focus of his life when he wrote Psalm 27. See if you can find what I'm talking about as you read it:

> *I have asked the Lord for one thing; one thing only do I want: to live in the Lord's house [presence] all my life, to marvel there at his goodness, and to ask for his guidance.*
> Psalm 27:4 GNT

Above all the things we could do *for* God, all the ways we could tell *about* God, He is most pleased with our pure desire to know Him, love Him and be with Him.

And, by the way, you may run into well-meaning people who tell you that you're excited now but that it will fade along with your passion. Please don't pay them any attention. What they are saying is usually rooted in their experience. God's design for our relationship with Him is that it would become increasingly more exciting, fulfilling and purposeful, not less.

A good parallel is marriage. Kris and I have been married nearly four decades, and we love each other more, are attracted more to one another and enjoy each other more than we ever have. And it continues to increase. When you choose to love another with all of your heart, your love doesn't fade over time; it flourishes!

I fall in love with my wife again and again. I fall in love with Jesus again and again. Let your love be a constant choice, and watch how it continuously increases!

LIVING WHAT YOU'RE LEARNING

Is any of this new to you? Are you used to thinking less about knowing God and more about going to church, not swearing, serving the homeless or giving money? One of the things that's helped me lock in this priority is this thought:

God doesn't need us;
He wants us.

Think about it. God can do everything Himself. In fact, He can do it better than if we're involved. God, who is all knowing, all powerful and owns the Earth, doesn't need anything from you or me. But He wants a relationship with us. Mind blowing! It's true. All through the Bible, we read about God, who is endlessly pursuing us, showing His love and giving us the opportunity to love Him in return.

Would you consider taking a moment and letting Jesus know how your thinking is changing? Would you tell Him you want to make knowing Him your top priority of living? I find when I jot a love note to God, it pleases Him to no end in the same way that a note from my son or daughter pleased me when they were little and barely able to write or spell.

Take time to sit back and think about what you've just read: God wants me to know Him intimately, the way best friends do. He knows me by name and loves me!

Here is space for you to write a note to Him. If you want, you can even draw Him a little picture on the next page, for His eyes only. Have fun.

Jesus,

MY DRAWING FOR GOD:

PRAYER

Lord Jesus, thank you for reminding us again of the great blessing of knowing You. Thank You for desiring such a relationship with each one of us. Teach the one reading these words to make this their top priority: knowing You and loving You. I ask this in Your beautiful name, Amen!

— STUDY GOD'S WORD, THE BIBLE —

I found myself going back and forth over whether to use the word "study" as part of this section's title. I realize not everyone likes to read. But we often find ourselves reading online, or in texts, or communicating via social media, or watching YouTube or various other ever-evolving ways of gaining knowledge. Reading a book may not be on the top of your list, and the thought of sitting down and diving into something as thick as the Bible can be very intimidating.

I want to ask God to help you begin to understand the depth of His love for you which He has expressed in the story that goes back to the creation of the world. The Bible is not only God's love letter to each of us, it's also His manual for living a good, abundant, meaningful, righteous life.

And, it's so much more.

The Bible is a written record of what God has said over centuries to His followers. This record is an expression of His heart through stories, poems, songs, parables and letters addressed to all of us.

For those not familiar with the Bible, here are some basic facts about the Bible:

- The Bible is a compilation of 66 separate books written by 40 writers.

- Although written by 40 writers, the Bible has only one author - God Himself.
- The Bible was written over a period of 1,500 years.
- The Bible has hundreds of prophecies about the future, and over 300 were fulfilled specifically in Jesus' life alone. (No other religion has a record of prophecies given and so accurately fulfilled.)
- The Bible is true, supernatural, alive and powerful.
- The Bible has been used by God to transform the lives of countless people.

The Bible describes itself as: the breath of God, the Word of God, bread of heaven and the sword of the Spirit. There are so many other ways to describe God's Word, so I'll sum things up by saying: the Bible is a book inspired by God, authored by God and written by people He supernaturally motivated. It is God's description of Himself so that we may start to understand Him. It is a declaration of His endless love for us, and, finally, it is His invitation to forgiveness and new life through the death of Jesus on the cross, and the entrusting of our lives to Him.

"But," you say, "the book is so big and so hard to understand that I don't even know where to begin!" Many people feel this way. I felt this way when I first started to read the Bible. It helped me when I learned that God was intimately involved in the process each time I opened it. As the author, He has the ability, through His Spirit, who now lives in you and me, to help us understand what He has written. He wants us to live a purposeful life of meaning, power and impact. His "life manual," the Bible, is the primary way He helps us learn and live abundantly. The following passage is a great description of what the Bible is designed to become to us:

> *There's nothing like the written Word of God for showing you the way to salvation through faith in Christ Jesus. Every part of Scripture is God-breathed and useful one way or another— showing us truth, exposing our rebellion, correcting our mistakes, training us to live God's way. Through the Word we are put together and shaped up for the tasks God has for us.*
>
> II Timothy 3:15–17 MSG

If the Bible is all of that and more, where's a person supposed to begin? This is a good question since the Bible is a compilation and not just a story that moves forward chronologically (in order).

My advice is to start with the four books which each describe the life of Jesus. By reading about Jesus and studying His life, you will get to know more about the One you've chosen to follow, as He will supernaturally speak to you.

How will He speak "supernaturally"? Here is what many people who experience His personal voice say as they read the Bible: "I felt the words jump off the page!" That's their way of describing Jesus revealing Himself, and His ways, in "real" time through this ancient but very alive text. The words they read come alive with meaning and application to their life.

You may have already experienced this when you were exposed to these words in the book of John:

> *God loved the world so much that he gave his only Son, so that everyone who believes in him would not be lost but have eternal life.*
>
> John 3:16 ERV

You may have realized God was saying He so loved you that He gave His only Son. For <u>you</u>, He gave Jesus, personally, sacrificially, sincerely. God loves <u>you</u>. God gave His all for <u>you</u>. You don't ever have to be lost, guilty or alone again! Now, if this **<u>one</u>** verse says so much to you, can you imagine what God wants to say in all 66 of the books that make up the Bible?

Are you ready to begin studying? Here are two ways to take your first steps into the Bible:

STEP ONE

Start with the four Gospels: *Matthew, Mark, Luke* and *John*. These four books of the Bible are narratives, or stories, and they are all about the same thing: Jesus' life, words, miracles, death and resurrection. "Why do I need to read the same story four different times?" Because the accounts are from four different followers of Jesus, and although they have a lot of the same parts of His life story, they each show unique things about Jesus' life. When you eventually read all four, you'll not only know more about Jesus, but if you read with an open and willing heart, you will actually know Him more. Remember, He's not only the subject of these four books, but through His inspiring Spirit, He's the author as well. Mind boggling, but true!

So, rather than reading all four at one time, I encourage you to start with the book of *John*. In the twentieth chapter, John actually tells us why he writes his book:

> *Jesus provided far more God-revealing signs than are written down in this book. These are written down so you will **believe** that Jesus is the Messiah, the Son of God, and in the act of **believing,** have real and eternal life in the way he personally revealed it.*
> John 20:30–31 MSG [emphasis added]

John was inspired by God to write so that everyone who reads would want to believe in Jesus, entrust their life fully to Him— just as you have—and then experience life and growth as God's new creation. Often, writers will emphasize a keyword in the books they write. In the book of *John,* the word that stands out most is *believe*. That makes sense since, in the passage above, John said this was his goal. But this might surprise you: he repeats the word *believe* in his book between 85 and 100 times, depending on the version you read.

Since *believe* (belief) is the goal of John's book, and since it's the keyword, it would be worthwhile to circle it every time you see it or to highlight on your Bible app. Then ask these three questions each time you find it:

1. **God, what were you saying to the people in the story about believing?**
   (possible observations you may have: that they believed after Jesus did something amazing; that they refused to believe; that they chose to oppose rather than believe, etc.)

2. **God, what are you saying to us today about believing You or believing in You?**
   (possible answers might be that I've started to believe, that Jesus is believable; that sometimes our fears or failures have kept us from believing; that Jesus loves people even before they believe, etc.)

3. **God, what are you saying to me, and how do you want me to apply what I'm learning to my life?**
   (possible answers: that you can trust Him with your life; that He will give you courage to believe enough to tell others about your love for Him and the life He offers; that there will always be people who oppose Jesus and belief in Him, but He's worth it, etc.)

Here is another way to describe these three simple steps: observation, interpretation and application. Observation is seeing what the passage says. Interpretation is understanding what the passage means. Application is applying the truth of the passage to my life.

Whether it's a single word or a full paragraph, this is a basic method for looking at every passage you read in the Bible. If you do this, and take your time to ponder and listen for God's Spirit, He will lead you in the study of His Word, and you will see your life change for the better.

LIVING WHAT YOU'RE LEARNING

Here is one of my favorite Bible stories, found in the book of *John*. It's a story of Jesus raising His friend Lazarus from the dead. If you are willing, I want you to read the entire passage. Then read it again, but this time circle the word *believe* each time you see it in the passage. (It's okay to write in your Bible or to highlight in your Bible app.) Next, take one *believe* at a time and answer the three questions I taught you. If you want to, you can write your answers down for each time *believe* appears, or you can type them into the notes section of your smartphone to review later. Go ahead and give it a try.

> *When Martha got word that Jesus was coming, she went to meet him. But Mary stayed in the house. Martha said to Jesus, "Lord, if only you had been here, my brother would not have died. But even now I know that God will give you whatever you ask."*
>
> *Jesus told her, "Your brother will rise again."*

"Yes," Martha said, "he will rise when everyone else rises, at the last day."

Jesus told her, "I am the resurrection and the life. Anyone who believes in me will live, even after dying. Everyone who lives in me and believes in me will never ever die. Do you believe this, Martha?"

"Yes, Lord," she told him. "I have always believed you are the Messiah, the Son of God, the one who has come into the world from God." Then she returned to Mary. She called Mary aside from the mourners and told her, "The Teacher is here and wants to see you." So Mary immediately went to him.

Jesus had stayed outside the village, at the place where Martha met him. When the people who were at the house consoling Mary saw her leave so hastily, they assumed she was going to Lazarus's grave to weep. So they followed her there. When Mary arrived and saw Jesus, she fell at his feet and said, "Lord, if only you had been here, my brother would not have died."

When Jesus saw her weeping and saw the other people wailing with her, a deep anger welled up within him, and he was deeply troubled. "Where have you put him?" he asked them.

They told him, "Lord, come and see." Then Jesus wept. The people who were standing nearby said, "See how much he loved him!" But some said, "This man healed a blind man. Couldn't he have kept Lazarus from dying?"

Jesus was still angry as he arrived at the tomb, a cave with a stone rolled across its entrance. "Roll the stone aside," Jesus told them.

But Martha, the dead man's sister, protested, "Lord, he has been dead for four days. The smell will be terrible."

Jesus responded, "Didn't I tell you that you would see God's glory if you believe?" So they rolled the stone aside. Then Jesus looked up to heaven and said, "Father, thank you for hearing me. You always hear me, but I said it out loud for the sake of all these people standing here, so that they will believe you sent me." Then Jesus shouted, "Lazarus, come out!" And the dead man came out, his hands and feet bound in graveclothes, his face wrapped in a headcloth. Jesus told them, "Unwrap him and let him go!"

Many of the people who were with Mary believed in Jesus when they saw this happen. But some went to the Pharisees and told them what Jesus had done. Then the leading priests and Pharisees called the high council together. "What are we going to do?" they asked each other. "This man certainly performs many miraculous signs. If we allow him to go on like this, soon everyone will believe in him. Then the Roman army will come and destroy both our Temple and our nation."

John 11:20–48 NLT

How'd you do? Did you find all of the believe words? You should have found a total of eight. Did you try answering the questions? Such an amazing story filled with loss and *unbelief,* with Jesus' hope and eternal life to those who *believe* (trust), with many people who saw what He did and *believed,* and with religious leaders (Pharisees) who tried to keep them from *believing.* Wow! All that in this little story! Can you see how this could apply to you and the situations in your life that seem hopeless, sad or dead?

PRAYER

Lord Jesus, help each person reading to understand how they can apply Your Word to their lives. Amen!

STEP TWO

The next step, after reading the four Gospels—and circling *believe* every time you see it in the book of *John*—is to get familiar with the resources available to help you study not only a passage of the Bible, but particular words in the Bible as well.

A quick Google search will render many online resources available to help you read from various versions, look up the many ways a particular word is used in the Bible (love, for example) and study what well-known theologians and commentators have said about each verse in God's Word.

The resources I would highly recommend are:

thebibleproject.com
This resource will give you a grasp of each book in the Bible as well as the Bible's major themes. And they have pictures, lots of them! I'm serious! Brief videos progressively, and artistically, draw out the contents of each book, and it's amazing.

They even have several videos, each less than eight minutes, that teach you how to study your Bible.

Bible (app) from Bible.com
This is a free Bible app in the app stores which provides many different versions of the entire Bible, daily reading plans and comments by scholars on every single verse. Check it out. By downloading, you have the entire Bible with you any time you have your mobile device.

RayMayhewOnline.com
Ray Mayhew is a close friend of mine. He is an amazing Bible teacher and a scholar, to boot. Plus, he's British. I don't know about you, but everything sounds better when it's spoken by someone with a British accent. Ray has taught on the content and meaning of every book of the Bible, and his website has audio recordings of each of his talks. It also has some more academic offerings for those who want to dive deeper. It's is a treasure trove of revelation. I hope you'll take some time to explore it.

LIVING WHAT YOU'RE LEARNING

I've spent quite a bit of time here on studying God's Word as a way to grow. I know it's a lot to take in. I hope that starting with John and focusing on a single word has shown you that you can read the Bible, and you can understand it, and, as you do, God will reveal more of Himself and His ways to you.

You may find other Christians talking about having "devotions" or "quiet time" and think, "What are they talking about?" I know I did. What those words simply mean are: time set aside daily to focus on knowing God, praying and reading His Word. This lets God know that He has our full attention and sets us up to stay connected with Him throughout our day.

Whether it's ten minutes with your coffee before you shower in the morning, or five minutes in your car on lunch break or twenty minutes at the end of your day, you are making time for you and God to meet.

I'll often begin this "quiet time" by telling Him how much I love Him and how thankful I am for my life, His love, my family and our church. Then, I will read a passage of the Bible, slowly and thoughtfully, reminding myself to ask: what was God saying to the people He wrote this to, what is He saying to us today, what is He saying to me and how do I apply what I'm learning?

I find it very helpful to have a journal to write down those answers, whether from His Word or from the whisper of His Spirit on my heart. I also write down my prayers to God as though I am writing Him a letter.

Try finding a _quiet_ time and see what happens. If you miss a day, don't beat yourself up. Most people strive for three or four times a week because life is so full. The more time you spend with Jesus, the more time you'll _want_ to spend with Him.

Let me round off this section with a promise for us from the Bible:

> _The truly happy person doesn't follow wicked advice, doesn't stand on the road of sinners, and doesn't sit with the disrespectful._
>
> _Instead of doing those things, these persons love the Lord's Instruction, and they recite God's Instruction day and night!_
>
> _They are like a tree replanted by streams of water, which bears fruit at just the right time and whose leaves don't fade. Whatever they do succeeds._
> Psalm 1:1–3 CEB

— DISCOVERING GOD'S WAYS —

In America, at least, almost everyone is familiar with the Lord's Prayer. They may even be able to recite some of it. It is a prayer Jesus taught His disciples. I learned it as a small boy but didn't begin to understand it until I was in my thirties. The part that most confused me was this:

Your kingdom come, your will be done,
on earth as it is in heaven.
Matthew 6:10 NIV

I had been taught that Jesus came to Earth to rescue me, die for me and provide me with eternal life. I would describe this as a _one dimensional_ view of God's plan for the world. I describe it this way because He has an even bigger plan and one that He's invited us to play an active role in.

God sent Jesus to our broken world to rescue us from the penalty of our sin, or spiritual cancer, and from its power in our lives. However, He doesn't stop there. God changes us so that we can be a part of His spiritual rescue effort (through our words, example and service). Here's one way Jesus describes our involvement:

> _You're here to be light, bringing out the God-colors in the world. God is not a secret to be kept. We're going public with this, as public as a city on a hill. If I make you light-bearers, you don't think I'm going to hide you under a bucket, do you? I'm putting you on a light stand. Now that I've put you there on a hilltop, on a light stand— shine! Keep open house; be generous with your lives. By opening up to others, you'll prompt people to open up with God, this generous Father in heaven._
> Matthew 5:14–16 MSG

I'm guessing one of the reasons you're reading this book is because someone shined the light and love of God on you by their good deeds and caring words. Am I right?

"Your Kingdom come, your will be done," is my agreement with God's agenda for planet Earth, which involves many more people than just me.

God's Kingdom, in simple terms, is God's plan, God's will, God's reigning presence and purpose. I know, it is still pretty big to take in. Here's another way of saying it:

God's Kingdom comes
any time God's plans are fulfilled in the lives of people.

Jesus' message, and what He continually taught His disciples, was that, "the Kingdom of God is among you." In other words, since Jesus came, made us **brand new** creations and put His abiding Spirit within us, His plans can now be fulfilled in and through our lives.

God wants you and me to be an important part of expressing His plans for Earth, as well as opposing the plans of another kingdom called the Kingdom of Darkness. It sounds like *Game of Thrones* or something, doesn't it? But this is for real.

There is a dark spiritual power which opposes God's plans and works to motivate people to live for themselves. You may have already run into this as you told your family or friends you have chosen to be a follower of Jesus, and they not only were uninterested but also were upset with you for doing this. The Dark Kingdom is one which opposes God being at the center, and places us on the throne instead of Him. It seeks to tighten our grip on the keys of our lives. This Dark Kingdom is the source of all heartache, pain, wars and death on Earth.

> *Yes, in the past your lives were full of those sins. You lived the way the world lives, following the ruler of the evil powers that are above the earth. That same spirit is now working in those who refuse to obey God.*
>
> Ephesians 2:2 ERV

God's plans for us not only include our salvation and the salvation of others, but also the transformation of the dark areas of life on Earth into areas of hope, provision, healing and peace. And all of us who follow Jesus are called to be a part of this transformation. We don't simply pray it; instead, we participate in His Kingdom coming. God wants to use _us_ to move planet Earth into partnership with Him. How, you ask? God wears people. What I mean is that God lives in us (wears us) to empower us to express His love and purposes to others.

"Your Kingdom come, your will be done, *on earth as it is in heaven.*" In heaven there is no spiritual cancer or death, so we are called to share the good news of God's salvation through faith in Jesus on Earth (by telling your story to your family, friends or co-workers of how you have experienced God's forgiveness and a real and personal relationship with Him). In heaven, there is no sickness, so we are called to bring healing on Earth (whether through prayer or building hospitals in hopeless nations). In heaven, there's no abuse, so we are called to stand up for those who are abused (whether by living among the marginalized, being a foster parent or being a part of the rescue of those caught in sex trafficking). In heaven, there is <u>no hunger</u>, <u>no poverty</u>, <u>no ignorance</u>, so we are called to provide food for the hungry, provision for those who lack basic necessities and education for all (whether it means distributing food and provision to refugees globally or the homeless locally or teaching basic reading skills to the poor).

It is God's will to work through you and me to see His Kingdom (heaven) come everywhere on Earth. He wants to use us to make a lasting difference on Earth by living out His Kingdom plans. He's not only interested in getting us to heaven, He's equally interested in getting heaven to us!

*I will **use you** to bless all the people on earth.*
Genesis 12:3 ERV [emphasis added]

*"Also, seek the peace and prosperity of the city to which I have carried you into exile. Pray to the Lord for it, because if it prospers, you too will prosper. . . For I know the **plans I have for you**,"* declares the Lord, *"plans to prosper you and not to harm you, plans to give you hope and a future."*
Jeremiah 29:7, 11 NIV [emphasis added]

*God saved you by his grace when you believed. And you can't take credit for this; it is a gift from God. Salvation is not a reward for the good things we have done, so none of us can boast about it. For we are God's masterpiece. He has created us anew in Christ Jesus, **so we can do the good things he planned for us** long ago.*
Ephesians 2:8–10 NLT [emphasis added]

*[Jesus said] Then the king will say to those on his right, "Come, you who will receive good things from my Father. Inherit the kingdom that was prepared for you before the world began. I was hungry and **you gave me food** to eat. I was thirsty and **you gave me a drink**. I was a stranger and **you welcomed me**. I was naked and **you gave me clothes** to wear. I was sick and **you took care of me**. I was in prison and **you visited me**."*
Matthew 25:34–36 CEB [emphasis added]

Jesus _did not_ come only to save us and bring a Saved-dom (just getting us saved for heaven). He came to bring a Kingdom. As our eyes are opened by God's Spirit, we begin to see our role, as well as the fierce opposition that wars against this Kingdom of selfless love and service.

This chart may help you see how vastly different life is when we are a part of God's Kingdom:

KINGDOM OF DARKNESS	VS.	HIS KINGDOM
HAPPINESS came from living for myself.		*HAPPINESS comes from living for God and others.*
LIFE was about how much I could get.		*LIFE is now about how much I can give.*
The goal in life is to be SERVED.		*The goal of life is to SERVE as Jesus did.*
When I get HURT, I get even!		*When I get HURT, I forgive, as Jesus forgave me.*
To have LIFE, I must grab it.		*To have LIFE, I must give it to God.*

When you decided to follow Jesus, you became an eternal citizen of the Kingdom of God. We are all citizens of some nation on Earth, but the Bible says that this is a temporary citizenship. While we are alive, we are dual citizens—Heavenly and Earthly— but our primary allegiance is to our eternal citizenship.

Our citizenship is in heaven. We look forward to a savior that comes from there—the Lord Jesus Christ. He will transform our humble bodies so that

they are like his glorious body, by the power that
also makes him able to subject all things to himself.
Philippians 3:20–21 CEB

Many Christians wrongly believe that becoming God's **brand new** creation is all about themselves. They miss God's greater agenda which Jesus and His followers spoke about and lived out: the Kingdom of God has arrived, live for the King (Jesus) and for His Kingdom.

However, it is good to remember that Jesus knows we have needs, bills, worries and schedules. So He gives us the key to seeing all those things met as we trust Him. Ready for this?

[Jesus said] Don't worry and say, "What will we
eat?" or "What will we drink?" or "What will
we wear?" That's what those people who don't
know God are always thinking about. Don't worry,
because your Father in heaven knows that you need
all these things. What you should want most is God's
kingdom and doing what he wants you to do. Then
he will give you all these other things you need.
Matthew 6:31–33 ERV

Another way to say this:

Focus on God and His Kingdom,
and He will take care of the rest.

LIVING WHAT YOU'RE LEARNING

One of the most profound examples of a person living to see God's Kingdom come to Earth is Mother Teresa. The little nun from Kosovo captured the attention of the entire world with her sacrificial service to the poor and dying of Calcutta, India.

She helped countless people and established a movement of compassion and God's manifest presence on Earth. Anyone might be intimidated by such a track record of service but not after reading some of her words:

> *"Not all of us can do great things. But we can do small things with great love."*
> —Mother Teresa

> *"Let no one ever come to you without leaving better and happier. Be the living expression of God's kindness: kindness in your face, kindness in your eyes, kindness in your smile."*
> —Mother Teresa

> *"I alone cannot change the world, but I can cast a stone across the waters to create many ripples."*
> —Mother Teresa

I've included these quotes because they emphasize a life of kindness expressed through God's love. This is not too difficult for any of us if we are willing to listen to God's Spirit speak within us.

Very often, the greatest hindrance to us bringing God's Kingdom to Earth is not a lack of faith but a lack of space. Our lives are so full, and we move at such a fast pace that we can miss the great needs all around us.

Take a moment and ask yourself a few questions:

1. Do you see a cashier who regularly seems sad? Have you considered praying for this person or saying something encouraging?

2. Do you have a neighbor who is not well-loved in your neighborhood because they are grumpy and maybe neglect to mow their lawn or rake their leaves? Have you ever thought about offering

to help or taking them cookies or just starting a conversation with them?

3. Do you have a friend or family member who would benefit from hearing the amazing changes you've experienced since you met Jesus? Someone, who like you, needs to begin a personal relationship with God? Why don't you start praying for them regularly, and ask God for an opportunity to share what He has done for and in you?

4. Do you know the various outreaches your local church offers, like the Open Door Mission for the homeless in Omaha, an orphanage in Costa Rica, organizations giving practical aid to refugees, etc.? Would you consider taking a step and finding out how God may want you to be a part?

5. Do you see work as just a grind in order to make money? Would you consider the idea that God may have you there as the only light in a dark place? Every time you smile at, share with and encourage your co-workers, you could be an expression of His Kingdom coming to Earth.

While reading these questions, the Spirit of God may be reminding you of people in your sphere of influence who need His love, His help and His salvation. This is a good time to pray for them and to ask God how He may want to use you to convey these things.

Now, take a moment and listen to God's quiet voice to see if there is something He would lead you to start _doing_ differently, and praying differently, this week. Write it below with the date, so that, when you look back, you'll be able to see how God is using you to see His Kingdom come, in your world, as it is in heaven.

PRAYER

Jesus, thank You for what You are doing in the life of Your new creation as they read and apply Your truth. Bless them with a great sense of Your presence and a sense of purpose as they express Your love to those around them. Give them courage to listen, to obey quickly, and then to expect You to do great things. Bless their lives. Remind them that You are with them and will never leave them! In Your name! Amen!

I hope what you are reading is helping you understand your life as God's new creation. You're bound to have questions, so I encourage you to be in touch with one of your Christian friends, your life group or one of your pastors who, I'm confident, will all be glad to help you.

CHAPTER 5
SHARE LIFE IN YOUR NEW COMMUNITY

Families are funny. Have you ever been to a family reunion where you actually felt as though you barely knew anybody? Have you been to one where you knew everybody but wish you didn't? How about one where everybody knew and loved each other—warts and all—and actually _wanted_ to be together?

I wish most of our experience with family was the latter.

FAMILY
A group of people, sharing the same DNA,
who know each other, love each other—warts and all—
and want to be together.

This isn't common because of the spiritual cancer you learned about earlier. Sin affects everything, including relationships. This is why some people, and some family members, are easier to love than others.

And, some are just hard to love at all.

The fact is, the only way people can get along and really love each other, family or not, is by becoming God's **brand new** creation through Jesus. When He comes to live inside us through His Holy Spirit, He begins to love <u>through</u> us in ways we could never have imagined.

> *For Christ's love compels us, because we are convinced that one died for all. . . **that those who live should no longer live for themselves but for him who died for them and was raised again.***
> II Corinthians 5:14–15 NIV [emphasis added]

When we choose to follow Jesus, He gives us His supernatural love. A perfect love. One that thinks the best, continually forgives, overlooks differences and gives selflessly. Believe me, I know the difference between my imperfect love and His. You will, too.

> *We love because he first loved us.*
> I John 4:19 NIV

I want to get really transparent here and talk about the elephant in the room. Most people you encounter every day have good thoughts about Jesus. They see Him as a great teacher, a peacemaker, a model to follow, someone who loves everyone, but most people don't have good thoughts about Christians or the Church as a whole. Has that been your experience?

Christian is often thought to mean: Republican, judgmental, homophobic, and hypocritical. **Definitely non-inclusive.**

Church is often seen as: a lifeless place, where lifeless people talk about irrelevant things and then go home more unfulfilled than when they came.

Unfortunately, these descriptions do apply to _some_ Christians and _some_ churches because we are broken people, part of an imperfect community, in the process of being made whole.

When you decided to follow Jesus, you were automatically adopted into His family forever. This is a huge family of Christians around the entire world called the _global_ Church. The congregation you may be a part of where you live would be the _local_ Church. They all love the same Jesus. Many, many of them are living for His Kingdom and don't reflect the unattractive description I gave previously. Here are a couple of descriptions that come closer to what a Christian and the Church ought to be:

Christian, a person who: (1) has decided to trust Jesus alone for their salvation and ultimate leadership of their life, (2) consistently, and without judgment, expresses God's love and purposes to everyone they encounter and (3) attracts and intrigues those seeking God or purpose in their life.

Church: I'll start with this definition by Eldon Babcock

*The Church in its essence is nothing less than a life-pulsating people who are **animated** by the indwelling presence of Jesus.*

The Church is really the imperfect people of God being transformed by Him, and empowered to express His love toward one another and those on their way to following Him. The way the people of Lifegate (the church I lead in Omaha) express this is:

We do life together.
We live in authentic, committed relationships where we can belong and experience real life in Jesus.

I hope you've encountered a real Christian. I'm guessing someone who loved Jesus played a role in you coming to know Him. I also hope you've experienced a church which is animated by the living presence of Jesus. If not, God is inviting you to be a part of one!

— YOUR NEW CREATION FAMILY —

I'm going to give you a few descriptions of what this new family, the Church, is and does. My reason? To help you see how important other followers of Jesus are to your growth. Don't get me wrong; I know few, if any of us have ever experienced a perfect family. But I want you to know that Jesus' vision for His family, which includes you, on Earth is perfect, and He is committed to help us experience it.

An Adopted Family

But to all who believed him and accepted him, he gave the right to become children of God.
John 1:12 NLT

*So you have not received a spirit that makes you fearful slaves. Instead, you received God's Spirit when he **adopted** you as his own children. Now we call him, "Abba, [Papa] Father."*
Romans 8:15 NLT [emphasis added]

Do you remember "picking teams" as a kid? All bunched together in the front yard while the "chosen two"—usually self-elected—decided everyone's fate with the cold wave of a finger.

I don't know about you, but, for me, this was tense. Without knowing it, I felt validated in my soccer abilities and in my value as a person when someone picked me. If I wasn't picked right away, or, worst of all, picked last, I felt like a loser who the better kids had to put up with.

Can you relate to this at all?

Being adopted into God's family in today's terms means: God picked you, and He did it in the first round! Why? Because He loves you and wants you on His team, in His family.

GOD PICKS YOU!

Even if your family said you were an accident, or you got passed over for a promotion or your spouse chose someone else to be with, God picks you and wants you forever and ever.

When you said "yes" to Jesus, the adoption was final! You're His, and you're in His family.

A Loving Family

We know what real love is because Jesus gave up his life for us. So we also ought to give up our lives for our brothers and sisters.
I John 3:16 NLT

*Dear friends, let us continue to **love one another,** for love comes from God. Anyone who loves is a child of God and knows God.*
I John 4:7 NLT [emphasis added]

I wish space permitted me to tell you all the ways my family and I have been loved by God's family. When my wife battled breast cancer for a second time—which required another round of chemo, a double mastectomy and numerous difficult surgeries—God's people rallied in every way imaginable. From praying, to providing meals, to giving money, to being a comforting presence. God's people were His very body. His hands, His voice, His tears, His care on our behalf.

Have you experienced the love of God's family? It's selfless, generous and free of strings.

At Lifegate Church, we tell people that they come "pre-loved." I love that little phrase. It means our love is not volatile, ebbing and flowing on the tide of our emotions. Instead, our love is a steadfast choice to care for and serve every person God brings to us.

We tell people, "We love you just the way you are, and we love you enough to help you grow into all you are meant to become."

I realize this all sounds good, but being a loving family of God doesn't happen overnight, and it definitely doesn't happen automatically.

It involves a commitment to love and not give up. It means we blow it and seek forgiveness, and we give forgiveness when others do the same. And, over time, we find ourselves starting to really love each other.

A Unified Family

Jesus prayed for you and me, right before He died on the cross. I know, this may be hard to believe, but it's true. You may be surprised by what He prayed and why.

> *I'm praying not only for them, But also for those who will believe in me, Because of them and their witness about me. The goal is for all of them to become* **one heart and mind**—*Just as you, Father, are in me and I in you, So they might be* **one heart and mind** *with us. Then the world might believe that you, in fact, sent me.*
>
> John 17:20–23 MSG [emphasis added]

Getting along with other Christians is a big thing with God. Of all the things Jesus could pray for before dying on the cross, He prayed for His family to be unified, of one heart and mind. Jesus is praying specifically for you and me.

Do you know what the number one complaint against Christians is? That they don't do what they say they believe. That they're hypocrites.

Do you know what the second complaint is? That they're always fighting and can't get along.

Too often, both of these complaints are completely accurate. But they don't have to be. When we decide to follow Jesus, He takes us by the hand and leads us on a journey. This journey involves a continuous series of choices to either live for Him or live for ourselves. The people in the world judge us on our track record of failures. I don't blame them. It makes sense. But I see a bigger picture and pray you can as well.

The world is waiting for Christians to get along, to stop competing, to love each other more than they love themselves. The life-giving churches in Omaha (where I live) provide a good example of this. The leaders have decided that what we all agree upon is more important than the theological things we disagree on. We have decided to take Jesus' prayer seriously and be an active part of its answer. Ron Dotzler, who founded the Abide Network in Omaha, says it best and says it over and over:

We are BETTER TOGETHER.

And it's happening. Churches are working together with the mindset that we cannot win unless other churches and Christians in our region win. We realize our greatest testimony to a hurting world—that Jesus is alive—is the way we love each other and unite our hearts and energies together.

This takes work. This takes a commitment to want Jesus' way more than our own. St. Augustine said something thousands of years ago that regularly inspires me when I'm tempted to focus on how other Christians, or churches in God's family, aren't quite like I am. He reminds us what really matters and how we should respond to the areas that don't matter:

In the essentials, UNITY
In the nonessentials LIBERTY
In all things CHARITY.

Another way to say this would be:

Stick together like Gorilla Glue on the things that matter most.
Don't sweat the things that don't, but give each other grace.
Above everything, what we believe or don't believe,
commit to unconditionally love and not judge.

Now, even though a "nonessential" may not ultimately matter, until someone sees it as a nonessential, they will defend or condemn it passionately. What do I mean?

I have a tattoo. Lots of people have tattoos. My tattoo isn't tiny. Having a tattoo bumps some people who love Jesus, and they let me know on Facebook. The result? An online divide between those who view the topic of tattoos as essential and those who view them as nonessential. And sometimes it's a bare-knuckle, Christian verbal brawl across the Internet.

All over a tattoo? Yep.

Over the centuries, the divide has been over covering your head at church (I know, for real?), using instruments for worship, speaking in tongues, women being able to do leadership stuff, wearing makeup, elders who are single or guys with long hair. People have fought over these issues. They've ended friendships over these issues. They've even killed each other verbally and sometimes physically over these _nonessential_ issues.

I know, it's hard to believe. It's also a good reason to avoid the temptation to make your nonessential view, _THE_ view.

As Gabe Lyon puts it, may we become people "who are known _for_ what we are for rather than what we are against." As this happens, those who have had a bad impression of Christians and church may find themselves intrigued with our lives of love and find themselves taking steps toward choosing to trust and follow Jesus.

146

There's another reason to be unified: our protection. We have an enemy. Remember the Kingdom of Darkness we discussed? That is led by Satan, the Devil (Isaiah 14:12; Luke 10:18; Matthew 25:41). He is actually a fallen angel who rebelled against God before the world was created, and now he leads other fallen angels called "demons."

I don't write this to creep you out, but I do want you to see the bigger picture.

Here's what the Bible says our enemy is trying to do to every follower of Jesus:

Stay alert! Watch out for your great enemy, the Devil. He prowls around like a roaring lion, looking for someone to devour. Stand firm against him, and be strong in your faith. Remember that your family of believers all over the world is going through the same kind of suffering you are.

I Peter 5:8–9 NLT

Lions, wolves, hyenas and other predators are always looking for a meal. They hunt in groups, and they study the animals they pursue. It's difficult for them to attack and take down prey that is closely joined with its herd. But when an animal is young, confused, afraid or simply foolish, the predator will single that one out to attack and devour. Our enemy, the Devil, is likened to a prowling lion checking out God's family to see if there are any beginners, any loners. any who are inexperienced, weak or not being cared for, any who are offended and have pulled away from others. He's patient; he's powerful, and unity is one of our greatest defenses against him.

When we are a unified family, the chances of the Devil overcoming any of us are very slim. May this motivate us to stick together and love one another, no matter our hurts, wounds, opinions or differences.

If no one has ever said this to you, let me be one of the first to welcome you to God's family. If you're a part of Lifegate Church, please know we are committed to love you, invest in your walk with God and stand with you as you experience the joys, losses, victories and disappointments in life. You're in a safe place now. And if we blow it—and we will—we'll strive to admit it quickly, seek your forgiveness sincerely and then move forward together.

An Active Family

The family that God has made us a part of actually DOES STUFF TOGETHER. Because we are the living expression of Christ's body on planet Earth, you can expect that we are doing all the things Jesus is doing.

Things such as bringing meals to new moms in the church or a shut-in next door, or going to a ball game together, or caring for refugees in Serbia or Lebanon or having a baby shower. God's people are on the move.

Here's how the Bible describes the first Church that assembled after Jesus ascended to heaven:

> *The believers spent their time listening to the teaching of the apostles. They **shared everything** with each other. They **ate together** and **prayed together.** Many wonders and miraculous signs were happening through the apostles, and **everyone felt great respect for God.** All the believers stayed together and shared everything. They sold their land and the things they owned. Then they **divided the money and gave it to those who needed it.** The believers shared a common purpose, and every*

day they spent much of their time together in the Temple area. They also ate together in their homes. They were happy to share their food and ate with joyful hearts. The believers praised God and were respected by all the people. **More and more people were being saved every day,** *and the Lord was adding them to their group.*

Acts 2:42–47 ERV [emphasis added]

But, Christians are not just active among themselves; that's only the starting point. God has called us to be involved in the common good of the people we live among in our city, our nation and the world. He calls us to be a "neighbors-and-nations people," who are making a difference by taking a stand for what is just and right and sacrificially serving those in need.

This is one of the reasons we at Lifegate try to encourage every person to take a journey across cultural and geographic lines, whether in our city or to other nations. We've seen God use this to unite our hearts and minds as we become a people with a "glocal" (global + local) assignment. Like the time the people of our church invested $107,000 into water purification systems for Burmese refugee children in Thailand, which is still providing clean water to thousands daily. Or our involvement and support of the Assure Women's Center in Omaha which played a key role in the rescue of over 1,600 unborn children in 2016. Or the teams we send to work with Afghan refugees in Greece or earthquake victims in Turkey.

We are God's united family making a difference in the world.

A Global and Growing Family

Our spiritual family members, followers of Jesus, are found in every nation around the globe. God's purpose is that His offer of life through Jesus, and His Kingdom, would come to all people, all cultures, in all nations. "For God so loved the world," in John 3:16 means people everywhere! Jesus' final commission to His followers was a global one:

Jesus, undeterred, went right ahead and gave his charge: "God authorized and commanded me to commission you: Go out and train everyone you meet, far and near, in this way of life, marking them by baptism in the threefold name: Father, Son, and Holy Spirit. Then instruct them in the practice of all I have commanded you. I'll be with you as you do this, day after day after day, right up to the end of the age."
Matthew 28:18–20 MSG

And when the Holy Spirit comes on you, you will be able to be my witnesses in Jerusalem, all over Judea and Samaria, even to the ends of the world.
Acts 1:8 MSG

What God has done in you by forgiving you, adopting you as His very own and putting His Spirit within you, He is doing all over planet Earth. This is the news you aren't likely to see on TV or read online.

I'm living proof of this global work! I gave my life to Jesus while living on the island of Taiwan, all because of the willingness of a neighbor to share how meeting Jesus transformed his life.

God cares for the world. I'm always amazed by the numerous examples of His supernatural pursuit of people to know Him.

I heard a story from my friend, Ray Mayhew, of how God is moving among refugees throughout the world. In 2016, Antioch

Church, of Waco, Texas, sent out 2,000 volunteers to work among the various refugees fleeing to Europe. Two of these volunteers found themselves on a ferry carrying about 500 refugees from the Island of Lesbos across the Aegean Sea to Greece. They struck up a conversation with one of the Syrian passengers fleeing for his life. Eventually, the man asked why the two volunteers were there. They explained that they were followers of Jesus who had sent them to show His care and compassion to the refugees.

The man said he had heard a little about Jesus and had even read some from the Injil (the Muslim word for Bible). He was deeply concerned with something though. Every night, for the past 90 nights, he had been visited by a bright figure whose face was so bright he couldn't even see its features. "Do you know who this is?" he asked the two relief workers.

They took him aside, where they could have a measure of privacy, and opened the Bible to the book of Daniel, Chapter 7:

> *His clothing was as white as snow, his hair like purest wool. He sat on a fiery throne with wheels of blazing fire, and a river of fire was pouring out, flowing from his presence. Millions of angels ministered to him; many millions stood to attend him.*
> Daniel 7:9–10 NLT

When they read this description to him, the Syrian man exclaimed, "That's him! Who is He?" After explaining that it was Jesus who had appeared to him, the man chose to put his faith in Christ alone and asked Him to become the Lord of his life.

Ninety nights in a row! God cared enough for this refugee that He appeared 90 nights in a row and then sent two relief workers, from Texas, to explain it! How awesome is that?!

You and I are a part of an adopted family, a loving family, a united family, a global and growing family. Might I add, it is an imperfect family. We are all at various places in our faith and growth. This requires a great amount of love, forgiveness and grace from one another if we are to become God's expression of love and presence on Earth.

> *Love from the center of who you are; don't fake it. Run for dear life from evil; hold on for dear life to good. Be good friends who love deeply; practice playing second fiddle. Don't burn out; keep yourselves fueled and aflame. Be alert servants of the Master, cheerfully expectant. Don't quit in hard times; pray all the harder. Help needy Christians; be inventive in hospitality. Bless your enemies; no cursing under your breath. Laugh with your happy friends when they're happy; share tears when they're down. Get along with each other; don't be stuck-up. Make friends with nobodies; don't be the great somebody.*
> Romans 12:9–16 MSG

I love this passage and hope it inspires you to commit to being a real Christian who loves God and loves others. Also, it's my prayer that you would be a part of a local church devoted to Jesus, filled with love for one another and making a difference in the world.

LIVING WHAT YOU'RE LEARNING

A man once told his friend, "I won't stop looking until I find the perfect church!" To which his friend replied, "Yeah, but if you start going to it, it won't be perfect any more."

I know most of you have been hurt by Christians, and by the "Church." If you are to ever experience God's plan for you, as a vital part of His global Church, it usually requires forgiveness of the bad examples you've encountered. It might be a junior high friend who tried to jam Jesus down your throat and kept telling you that you were going to hell. It might be the priest in your parish or a youth leader who was found to be immorally involved with a parishioner. It might be that the church you once attended made it clear you were under-dressed and over-tatted.

The list could be long or short.

God's desire is for no person or institution to keep us from following Him. When we forgive someone, we aren't saying, "What they did, or didn't do, is okay." Instead, we are saying, "What they did was wrong, but I choose to no longer hold an offense against them. I forgive and release them to God."

That's a tall order, I know.

Before we go any further, I want to ask for your forgiveness.

What?

You read right.

As a Christian and a pastor, I want to ask you to forgive _me_ for the things other followers of Jesus have said to you, said about you, done to you or failed to do for you. All the things which didn't reflect the Jesus they claimed to follow. They were wrong, and, on their behalf, I say, "I was wrong because I, too, am an imperfect follower of Jesus."

Would you forgive me?

> Instead, be kind to each other, tenderhearted, **forgiving one another,** just as God through Christ has forgiven you.
> Ephesians 4:32 NLT [emphasis added]

What motivates us to forgive? Note the words above: _just as God through Christ_ has forgiven you. Forgiveness is a supernatural gift from God. When we step out in faith, He will help us choose to forgive.

I know this is a painful process; I've had to go through it myself. To help you take even more specific steps, I've provided a space for you to record your forgiveness of me, as I represent those who have hurt you.

Are you ready to try? As I write this, I'm praying that God will reveal how close He is right now as you consider this step. Don't be surprised if your mind is flooded with faces of people or situations you haven't thought of for years. That's the Holy Spirit bringing them to memory so that, through your act of forgiveness, you can start to heal inside, as well as be set free from the harm they did to you or your family.

You may even be reading this through tears. I grieve with you. We, Christians and the Church, have all failed one another so many times. On the next page is a prayer for you to declare your forgiveness.

Start by listing individual Christians, leaders or churches who have wounded you.

Names of individuals, leaders or churches:

....

....

....

....

....

Now, pray this prayer and insert the list above into the appropriate spaces in the prayer.

PRAYER

Dear God,

Thank you for leading me to read this book so I can ask forgiveness of those who have hurt me so deeply. I choose to forgive as an act of obedience toward you and commitment to my new spiritual family.

I also want to confess my deep hurts, disappointments, wounds and offenses caused by those I've listed above.

I choose today, as an act of my obedience to your Word, to forgive each one and release them to You.

I forgive _____

for _____ .

and ask you to heal my heart, my memory and my life. Please release me from their offense as I let it go.

I also confess my unforgiveness to You and ask for Your ongoing mercy and forgiveness. Thank You for hearing my prayer.

In Jesus' name. Amen! (So be it!)

Now, let me pray for you:

Jesus,

*Thank You for being right here with my sister or brother
as they pray this powerful prayer of forgiveness.*

Begin a miracle of freedom and healing in their life.

*Show them how to live a lifestyle of forgiveness
which You modeled to us in Your life and sacrificial death.*

*I pray You would help them be a real, loving,
non-judgmental, faithful follower of You.*

*I ask also that You would place them in a church
where they belong, are loved and are needed
as a valued member of that community.*

*Thank you for their courageous obedience.
I pray blessing and strength and peace on their life.*

In Jesus' mighty name! Amen!

Whew! That was powerful. I'm confident you're feeling His presence and peace as you read and pray.

Each of the *Living What You're Learning* sections provides real time practice in the areas you'll live out as a Christ-follower. With each step, you are growing as God's **brand new** creation! I am proud of you. I know He's proud of you as well.

As I close out this section on the importance of sharing life in community, I want to encourage you to connect with those in your church who will walk with you through the process you've started. Forgiveness is indeed a process. We forgive, and when we remember the hurt, we forgive again and again until we can bless those who hurt us. At Lifegate, and at many life-giving churches, we have ministry teams that are available at the end of each weekend service, at every campus. They will help you walk out your decision to forgive and will also suggest other steps toward healing and wholeness.

YOUR IMPACT

CHAPTER 6
SHOW AND TELL

As someone who is experiencing a ***brand new life,*** you've probably noticed you want to tell everyone what God has done for you. This is because you have the best news on Earth: People can have a real relationship with God by trusting in and entrusting all to Jesus as their Savior and Lord.

Some hesitate to share, for fear of not having all the right words or methods. I want to encourage you to relax and look for opportunities to tell what Jesus has done for you. And when the Spirit leads, ask someone if they'd like to trust Jesus as well.

You're thinking, it can't be that simple!? It is.

Notice what Jesus says to a man after giving him forgiveness, salvation and freedom. The man desperately wanted to tag along with Jesus and His disciples, but instead, Jesus said:

Jesus did not let him, but said, "Go home to your own people and tell them how much the Lord has done for you, and how he has had mercy on you."
Mark 5:19 NIV

Jesus' Spirit lives in each one of us to lead us and give us wisdom and courage to be able to tell everyone how much He has done for us. So when you are sharing with someone, you are never alone.

When I was in the fifth grade, I lived in Monterey, CA with my family. I was—and still am—such an outdoors kid. I loved catching stuff. In the surrounding wooded hills, I'd look under damp, mossy logs and wrangle tiny little salamanders and things.

One day in particular, I caught something huge: an alligator lizard. Unlike so many other things I'd caught, he bit! I mean, he bit <u>hard</u>. If I had let him hold onto my thumb and shake his body, he would've drawn blood.

I was so proud of my alligator lizard that I wanted everyone to see it. I showed my brothers over and over. I showed my parents until they were sick of it. Then "show and tell" week at school rolled around, and I knew it was my time to shine. (I know, <u>isn't fifth grade a little old for show and tell</u>? To be clear, it wasn't called that but it was basically the same thing.)

I was ecstatic. I wanted everyone to see the amazing creature I'd caught, and I decided to even let it bite me on the finger, in front of everyone, even if it drew blood, just to show how cool he was.

I took the lizard to school; I held it up, and, to the awe, screams and delight of the entire class, it crunched onto my thumb.

Ahhhhh! Such a great memory. We're all adults now, but I believe if my classmates think back, they may actually remember the commitment, bravery and insanity of the kid who brought the alligator lizard for show and tell—and offered himself up as food.

Did you know God calls everyone who follows His Son, Jesus, to _show and tell_?

You won't find that phrase in the Bible, but you will find the word _baptism_. To Baptize basically means to submerge something completely under water and then bring it up again.

In Jesus' day, this act was done publicly to declare that someone had "let go" of their life (by allowing another person to put them under the water) and been raised to new life through Jesus' resurrection (that person lifts them back up out of the water).

Baptism is God wanting us to "show and tell" publicly that we have let go of our lives and now live to love and follow Him.

I'm going to share a few passages in the Bible where God is commanding us to be baptized, and then I'll explain the amazing object lesson He has designed it to be. Take your time reading the verses. And if you want, you can even turn to the passage in your Bible, or on your app, and read the story surrounding the verses to help you understand it even more.

*When all the people were being **baptized,** Jesus was baptized too. And as he was praying, heaven was opened and the Holy Spirit descended on him in bodily form like a dove. And a voice came from heaven: "You are my Son, whom I love; with you I am well pleased."*

Luke 3:21–22 NIV [emphasis added]

*Jesus, undeterred, went right ahead and gave his charge: "God authorized and commanded me to commission you: Go out and train everyone you meet, far and near, in this way of life, marking them by **baptism** in the threefold name: Father, Son, and Holy Spirit. Then instruct them in the practice of all I have commanded you. I'll be with you as you do this, day after day after day, right up to the end of the age.*

Matthew 28:18–20 MSG [emphasis added]

*Whoever believes and is **baptized** will be saved. But those who do not believe will be judged guilty.*

Mark 16:16 ERV [emphasis added]

*Peter replied, "Each of you must repent of your sins and turn to God, and be **baptized** in the name of Jesus Christ for the forgiveness of your sins. Then you will receive the gift of the Holy Spirit.*

Acts 2:38 NLT [emphasis added]

For you were buried with Christ when you were **baptized.** *And with him you were raised to new life because you trusted the mighty power of God, who raised Christ from the dead.*
Colossians 2:12 NLT [emphasis added]

These are just a few times in the Bible we are called to believe (trust Jesus fully) and then show it by being baptized.

We said earlier that baptism was God's call for every believer to show and tell their commitment publicly. Let me answer a few questions you may have in order to help you better understand this ancient and important act of obedience.

1. **Does a person have to be baptized in order to know God's salvation and go to heaven?**
   No. Just as putting a wedding ring on doesn't make a person married, baptism doesn't save a person. But in our culture, we wear a wedding ring to show everyone we're _taken for life,_ and baptism is the testimony to everyone that we have chosen Jesus and will live for Him alone. Baptism is an outward show of an inward commitment and change.

2. **If I was already baptized as a baby, do I have to do it again?**
   Yes, and here's why I believe this. In the Bible, baptism is always a decision by a person who has entrusted their life to Jesus. It is never something

that someone else decided for them. I know this may be difficult to grasp, especially if you've been raised in a tradition where the family all gets together, the baby is beautifully dressed, the pastor or priest pours water on their head, etc. I'm not putting any of that down, but want to do what the Bible tells us to do: Believe and then _choose_ to be baptized.

3. **I thought I'd given all the keys to Jesus when I was in High School, and even got baptized. But then I went on living my own way and hadn't given Jesus full control of my life. I've finally done that, and know I'm His new creation. Should I be baptized again**?
    Yes. I encourage anyone who knows that Jesus has saved them from the penalty of their spiritual cancer, and has resolved to follow and obey Him, to be baptized at that time _once and for all_.

4. **My family is having a real problem with me being baptized into my church because they are from a different tradition. Should I wait until they are convinced?**
    No. The reason we are baptized is to obey God, and to declare to others that we will do whatever He says. Jesus actually called us to be willing to leave the traditions and desires of our family in order to be a part of His family (Luke 14:26). This might surprise you, but many times God uses this

courageous act of obedience to actually create curiosity in our family and friends. A curiosity He uses to draw them to a real experience of faith in Jesus. And by the way, this isn't a baptism into a particular church or denomination, but in the name of the Father, Son and Holy Spirit.

5. **If I have put my full trust in Jesus alone for my forgiveness and salvation, but fell back into a sin, but now have forsaken it (repented) and am obeying Jesus again, do I need to be baptized again? (In other words, if I mess up bad and then ask God's forgiveness, would I need to be baptized each time?** No, and here's why. It's one thing to believe you have surrendered to Jesus and experienced no change because you hadn't given all your keys (see #3), and it's another thing to have given all and then allowed a sin in your life. When we hurt each other, my wife and I don't go out and buy another wedding ring to apologize. The ring is the testimony that we are committed to each other, and when we blow it, we make things right and keep moving forward in love—also, there are not enough credit cards in the world to float all _that_ precious metal. Our initial choice to commit everything to Jesus is followed by daily choices to follow Him. Baptism is the testimony, the declaration of the initial choice.

6. **I have a problem with a fear of water. It terrifies me. Does this mean I can never be baptized?**
No. At Lifegate we would first want to find out why you have the fear, in order to help you work through it and be healed. However we wouldn't let that hinder you from being baptized. Rather than putting you under water, we would pour water carefully over your head and shoulders.

I hope these answers are helpful to you. If I didn't answer a question you still have, ask one of the leaders in your church, and they'll help you find the answer.

— WHY GOD CHOSE BAPTISM AS THE ACT —

You may be like many people and ask, "What's the big deal about having someone else dunk you under water?"

I hope this begins to help you understand. God is a good teacher. He knows we need to go beyond saying we are committed and _show_ that we are committed. Baptism is one of the first and simplest things we can "do" and only requires that we find some water. He's also a teacher who gives great object lessons using everyday situations and objects (birds, flowers, bread, wine).

The Greek word (the language the New Testament of the Bible is written in) for baptism is "baptizo" which was a term the people in Jesus' day used to describe immersing or dunking something completely under water. It was also a term commonly used by those who dyed clothing. They would take a section of cloth and fully immerse (baptize) it into the vat containing the dye so that, when it came out, the entire cloth had a different color.

We immerse fully when we baptize. This is an expression of the object lesson of someone that is completely covered and completely changed, just like the cloth that was dyed.

But, the pool of water, the immersion and the resurfacing have even more meaning. Here are several things a person is experiencing, by faith, when they are baptized.

The water represents our death and burial.

I know, that sounds kind of gross, but let me explain. In civilized countries, when a person dies, we bury them. When you and I choose to follow Jesus, we have decided to die to our own way, die to ourselves and follow Him. Just as He gave His life up for us, we give our lives up by faith to follow Him.

> In our baptism we shared in his death. So when we were baptized, we were buried with Christ and took part in His death. And just as Christ was raised from death by the wonderful power of the Father, so we can now live a new life.
>
> Romans 6:4 ERV

The water represents our total cleansing.

When people take a bath, it's usually because they want to cleanse the entire body. When we chose Jesus, we didn't ask Him to cleanse us from half of our sins, or 80% of them, but all of them. Being fully immersed under water shows that, as water cleanses our entire physical body, the blood of Jesus has cleansed our entire spiritual body.

But if we are living in the light, as God is in the light,
then we have fellowship with each other, and the
*blood of Jesus, his Son, cleanses us from **all** sin.*
I John 1:7 NLT [emphasis added]

The water represents our resurrection to a new life.

People who have become a **brand new** creation in God now live by God's Spirit—His power. The Bible calls this "resurrection power" because it is the power God used to defeat the grave and raise Jesus from the dead.

When you are lifted out of the water, you are declaring to everyone that the old person, the self-focused one, is dead and that your new person is alive in Jesus. Just as Jesus rose from the grave, you are demonstrating the reality that you also have been raised from the dead spiritually.

Christ died, and we have been joined with him by
*dying, too. So we will also be **joined with him by***
***rising from death** as he did. We know that our old*
life was put to death on the cross with Christ. This
happened so that our sinful selves would have no
power over us.
Romans 6:5–6 ERV [emphasis added]

I identified myself completely with him. Indeed,
*I have been crucified with Christ. **My ego is no***
***longer central.** It is no longer important that I*

appear righteous before you or have your good opinion, and I am no longer driven to impress God. Christ lives in me. The life you see me living is not "mine," but it is lived by faith in the Son of God, who loved me and gave himself for me.
Galatians 2:20–21 MSG [emphasis added]

*I also pray that you will understand the incredible greatness of God's power for us who believe him. This is **the same mighty power** that raised Christ from the dead. . .*
Ephesians 1:19–20 NLT [emphasis added]

Are you starting to see how powerful our simple act of baptism is?

So many profound realities are being expressed when we choose to obey Jesus and follow His example by declaring to the world:

> *Jesus is now my Lord! I've died to myself,*
> *I am cleansed from all sin by His blood, and*
> *will love Him and live for Him from now on!*

By the way, the person baptizing you will give you the opportunity to express your allegiance to Jesus when you get baptized by declaring "Jesus is Lord of My Life!" We do this because the Bible encourages us to "go public" with our faith.

Paul describes this act in his letter to the Romans:

> *If you openly declare that Jesus is Lord and believe in your heart that God raised him from the dead, you will be saved. For it is by believing in your heart that you are made right with God, and it is by openly declaring your faith that you are saved.*
> Romans 10:9–10 NLT

Let me ask you some questions.

- Do you see why God wants all of us to be baptized?
- Are you starting to see the kinds of realities you declare when you get baptized?
- Have you chosen to die to the old you and, through Jesus, become the new you?
- Is Jesus your choice as the Lord, the leader of your life?
- Have you been baptized?
- Is there any reason why you should wait?

LIVING WHAT YOU'RE LEARNING

God's "show and tell" act of baptism is not only an expression of all the things we've talked about; it is also a *defining moment,* a rite of passage, if you will. And God is there to do something supernatural in you as you obey Him.

Over the years, I've been a part of thousands of people being baptized, and many things happen when people are baptized. Some are set free from sins that still held onto them. Others are healed of physical or emotional wounds. Some who've been gripped by spiritual darkness are delivered, and, finally, joy, peace and confidence well up in the hearts of those who obey in this way.

Hopefully, this chapter has inspired you to follow Jesus into the water of baptism, an expression of going public with your love for, and commitment to Him. Whether you are at Lifegate or a part of another congregation, I'm confident you can find information about baptism preparation and events on the church website. Why not take a moment to look and sign up right now?

Life is busy, I know. This act of obedience is so powerful that you'll want to follow through as soon as possible. It's time for _show and tell!_

Once you've been baptized, why not come back to this chapter and write down the date and what you experienced?

Baptism Date/Location:

_____

_____

MY BAPTISM EXPERIENCE

CHAPTER 7
LIVING FULLY CHARGED

You might be thinking at this point in the book: _I never knew becoming God's **brand new** creation was so amazing and yet so complex_. Knowing God is a relationship, and relationships are beautifully complex!

The truth is, following God requires learning to live in an entirely different reality. An eternal, supernatural reality. The Bible actually tells us that the realm of the spirit is lasting and _real_ and that the natural realm is temporary. Unfortunately, far too many people focus on the temporary and find it doesn't satisfy their deepest longings. This is because we are eternal beings.

> _So we fix our eyes not on what is seen, but on what is unseen, since what is seen is temporary, but what is unseen is eternal._
> II Corinthians 4:18 NIV

[Jesus said] You won't be able to say, "Here it is!" or "It's over there!" For the Kingdom of God is already among you.
Luke 17:21 NLT

Though we are still in this physical world, we are also part of a supernatural, spiritual world. Our joy, and assignment, as followers of Jesus is to welcome His supernatural salvation, love, deliverance, healing, presence and power into the world we live in.

The Apostle Paul gives a tremendous description of the two worlds forming our new reality. Here, he talks about our ability to stand against the devil's tactics:

The world is unprincipled. It's dog-eat-dog out there! The world doesn't fight fair. But we don't live or fight our battles that way—never have and never will. The tools of our trade aren't for marketing or manipulation, but they are for demolishing that entire, massively corrupt culture. We use our powerful God-tools for smashing warped philosophies, tearing down barriers erected against the truth of God, fitting every loose thought and emotion and impulse into the structure of life shaped by Christ.
II Corinthians 10:3–6 MSG

If this sounds superhuman, it's because it's supernatural.

Do you have a favorite superhero?

I have several. I have to make one thing clear, up front, before I take the superhero example any further. Here goes:

Superheroes aren't real.
They are make-believe.

I know, we want them to be real, but they aren't.

Iron Man is one of my favorites. Not Tony Stark, the self-centered, ego-driven main character, but Iron Man, the superhero who fights with superhuman power against the forces of evil. If you've not seen the movies, here is the very short version of how Iron Man came to be.

An explosion sends shrapnel into Tony's heart, threatening to kill him as it gradually moves deeper. Surgery was out of the question. It was hopeless. He was going to die.

Unless, somehow his heart could be protected.

Enter the *arc reactor,* a nuclear implant surgically placed directly in the middle of his chest to halt the shrapnel's inward travel. It saved his life; actually, it changed his life.

It was as though he had a "born again" experience, a new view of what mattered in life. The result? He built a sweet iron suit that fit over every part of his body. This suit was powered by the very *arc reactor* inside of him.

Behold, the Iron Man! Champion of good against the forces of evil. He was now a superhero with superpowers.

This is a description of what God said He was going to do in, and for, every person infected with spiritual cancer. See if this sounds at all like Iron Man:

> *I'll pour pure water over you and scrub you clean.*
> *I'll give you a new heart, put a new spirit in you. I'll*
> *remove the stone heart from your body and replace*
> *it with a heart that's God-willed, not self-willed. I'll*
> *put my Spirit in you and make it possible for you to*
> *do what I tell you and live by my commands.*
> Ezekiel 36:25–27 MSG

Shocked? God promised thousands of years ago to send Jesus and replace our terminal heart with a **brand new**, clean, powerful and eternal heart. But, unlike the Iron Man story, this is one is real.

Many of you reading are actually experiencing this new heart, the heart of Jesus in you.

Here's how the New Testament describes this transfer:

> *Then Christ will make his home in your hearts as*
> *you trust in him. Your roots will grow down into*
> *God's love and keep you strong.*
> Ephesians 3:17 NLT

Now, stick with me. God put His supernatural heart in us when we trusted His Son. Remember earlier, when we learned that Jesus promises the Spirit—God living in us and through us:

> *You can tell for sure that you are now fully adopted as his own children because God sent the Spirit of his Son into our lives crying out, "Papa! Father!" Doesn't that privilege of intimate conversation with God make it plain that you are not a slave, but a child?*
>
> Galatians 4:6–7 MSG

But, God has more planned for us. He puts His Spirit **in us** to release life when we trust Jesus, and soon after we make that decision, He wants to put His Spirit **on us** to release power.

Remember the Iron Man analogy?, Tony had the arc reactor placed **in** him to experience a whole new life, and then he had the Iron Man suit placed **on** him to express superhero power and action. Did you catch those two words?

IN and ON

God does something very similar for every believer, but, as I mentioned earlier: what God does is not make-believe; it's for real.

Would you take your time and read through the following verses? They describe this process of God's Spirit coming ON us and why He does this:

And the Spirit of the Lord came powerfully **upon** *David from that day on.*

I Samuel 16:13 NLT [emphasis added]

One day when the crowds were being baptized, Jesus himself was baptized. As he was praying, the heavens opened, and the Holy Spirit, in bodily form, descended **on him** *like a dove. And a voice from heaven said, "You are my dearly loved Son, and you bring me great joy.*

Luke 3:21–22 NLT [emphasis added]

But the Holy Spirit will come **on you** *and give you power. You will be my witnesses. You will tell people everywhere about me—in Jerusalem, in the rest of Judea, in Samaria, and in every part of the world.*

Acts 1:8 ERV [emphasis added]

Then Paul laid his hands on them, and the Holy Spirit came **on them.**

Acts 19:6 ERV [emphasis added]

We could spend a lot more time looking at amazing passages where God's Spirit came powerfully _on_ people, but I want to move us to the why.

This is an oversimplification, but it has helped me understand the difference between IN and ON:

God's Spirit comes **IN** us, for us, to become spiritually born again, a ***brand new*** creation and to know we are His very own forever. Our terminal heart becomes an eternal heart.

God's Spirit comes **ON** us, for others. He (the Spirit) empowers us to live a supernatural life of love and to offer the possibility of a relationship with God to others—a relationship with power to live above and beyond losses, failures and wounds.

> *The Spirit*
> *comes **IN us** for us and*
> *comes **ON us** for others.*

Watch this:

> *After they had prayed, the meeting place shook. They were <u>all filled with</u> the Holy Spirit and <u>bravely spoke</u> God's message.*
> Acts 4:31 CEV [emphasis added]

All through the Bible, and especially when Jesus shows up in the New Testament, we see the Holy Spirit coming <u>on</u> the people God loves with supernatural and real power.

Now, I have to admit this confused me for a long time. If the Holy Spirit comes to live ***inside*** of us, then why can't all of His work be an inside job? Why does He have to come ***upon*** us?

I don't know.

There, I said it. I really don't know, but I know He does.

Here's one way to think about it that might help. My wife and I are married. We are now one in spirit according to God's Word (Mark 10:8), but this doesn't mean our marriage is healthy, loving and growing. We can live in the same house (as one) but be distracted by children, bills, home maintenance or our love for football or shopping. We can be neglectful and find our marriage lacking intimacy, closeness or the tangible presence of God.

We are *"in"* the house together but ***not*** "on" the same frequency.

Does that help a bit? If not, don't worry. He, the Spirit, is going to lead you to the truth and the explanation you need most to help you understand. Jesus promised.

When the Spirit of truth comes, He will guide you into all truth.

> *I have much more to say to you, but right now it would be more than you could understand. The Spirit shows what is true and will come and guide you into the full truth.*
> John 16:12–13 CEV

This chapter is titled "Living Fully Charged." I'm trying to convey that God's plan is not only to put His Spirit ___in___ us, for us, but also ___on___ us, to release all of His supernatural power into our lives. In real terms, we don't live this **brand new** creation life by our power but through His.

I can't begin to tell you how important this is. Second only to God's Spirit coming **_in_** us, to cause us to become a new creation, is the Spirit of God coming **_on_** us as He did on Jesus at His baptism. This empowers us to do everything.

> *But the Holy Spirit*
> *will come _on_ you and give you power.*
> Acts 1:8 ERV [emphasis added]

If you're zoning out, I get it. Take some time away to mull over what you've just read: **IN** and **ON,** etc.

Maybe go watch *Iron Man.*

Here are three BIG IDEAS to help you understand and experience the Spirit's FULL CHARGE!

1. WE ARE MADE TO BE DEPENDENT ON A POWER SOURCE

This shouldn't surprise us that much. Most of the tools we use to interact, work and relate with every day are dependent on being charged up or fueled up. From cars to smart-phones to lawn mowers, we depend on power for just about everything.

All the way back in the Old Testament, God makes it clear that our spiritual life and power come from His Spirit.

> *'Your help will not come from your own strength and power. No, your help will come from my Spirit.'*
> *This is what the Lord All-Powerful says.*
> Zechariah 4:6 ERV [emphasis added]

This is not a natural power source; it's supernatural and limitless.

> *And you will know that God's power is very great for us who believe. It is the same as the mighty power He used to raise Christ from death...*
> Ephesians 1:19–20 ERV

Tony Stark had his imperfect Iron Man suit; we have the perfect Holy Spirit come <u>upon</u> us for real power in real life!

2. BEING FULLY CHARGED IS A CHOICE

Hopefully, you are starting to see that everything in your new life as a follower of Jesus is a choice which involves faith. You choose to entrust your life to Jesus, by faith. You choose to obey or disobey him, by faith. You also choose whether or not you are willing to have God's Spirit come upon you with power, also by faith. In other words, being filled with the Spirit of God is not automatic.

The Spirit doesn't want to possess you (controlling you without your choice), but wants to partner with you to see God's Kingdom come on Earth. This still blows my mind!

The Spirit is about
PARTNERSHIP, not POSSESSION.

The vast majority of us have smartphones. As a matter of fact, I'm guessing your phone is somewhere this very moment where you can see it, feel it or hear it. Mine is on the armrest of the chair I'm sitting in as I write these words.

For the sake of understanding fully charged, let's say the smartphone represents you.

Before you purchased your smartphone, it rested in a neat little box. Though having great potential, the device was dead. Dead because it hadn't been bought and connected to service via Sprint, AT&T, Verizon, etc.

Like a smartphone, you and I were born with astounding potential, gifts and passions. But the Bible says we were dead spiritually. This is tragic. We were made in the image of God, to know God and live with eternal purpose and impact. But until Jesus makes us His **brand new** creation, we are lifeless.

That is until we take a step of faith and choose.

The moment we chose to follow Jesus, we were connected to heaven and came alive. We received cell service. We didn't have to do anything but choose to trust fully. Do you see it? Jesus set up an eternal plan, and connected you with the one-time payment of His blood which resulted in an eternal connection with God.

We knew our smartphone worked because, once connected, the screen turned on, and we saw functioning apps. In our case, we knew we became hooked up to God because the Holy Spirit wrote it on the message board of our hearts. God told us we belong to Him, and He was now _in_ us—just as the smartphone showed that service was now working in the phone when we connected it to a plan.

We are alive. We are a new creation. We are connected with heaven. The Spirit is in us but . . .

The first thing you must do when your smartphone service gets connected, is to _fully_ charge your phone. This is essential for the phone to function with lasting power; otherwise, it will just lie dormant. It'll have service; it'll have potential, but it won't have any juice.

Does this sound vaguely familiar? Remember what we just read:

> 'Your help will not come from your own strength
> and power. No, your help will come _from my Spirit_.'
> This is what the Lord All-Powerful says.
>   Zechariah 4:6 ERV [emphasis added]

In the same way, we are designed by God to require *a full charge* if we are to live through the power of His Spirit and not our own strength.

This fires me up because I've lived long enough to know just how far my own strength gets me. The Bible even tells us how limited we are but how able He is!

> *Surely you know the truth. Surely you have heard. The Lord is the God who lives forever! He created all the faraway places on earth. He does not get tired and weary. You cannot learn all he knows. He helps tired people be strong. He gives power to those without it. Young men get tired and need to rest. Even young boys stumble and fall. But those who trust in the Lord will become strong again. They will be like eagles that grow new feathers. They will run and not get weak. They will walk and not get tired.*
> Isaiah 40:28–31 ERV

Our power to live for Jesus comes from an initial, full charge from the Holy Spirit which happens when He comes **on us** the first time.

This is what happened to Jesus at His baptism when the Spirit came *upon* Him like a dove. This is what happened in the book of Acts, Chapter 2, when the 120 or so followers of Jesus experienced the Spirit coming *upon* them with power and sending them out to spread the news of Jesus. This is what happened to the Apostle Paul after he encountered Jesus on the road to Damascus, was struck blind, then healed and filled with the Spirit of God in Acts 9.

This is also what happened to me. I had met Jesu and was trying to follow Him as best I could, but I lacked power, boldness and love.

During the first year of my decision to follow Jesus, I picked up two hitchhikers one day outside of Washington, DC. Their car had broken down (let me make it clear that I'm not encouraging you to pick up hitchhikers unless clearly led by God's Spirit). I could tell right away they were followers of Jesus by the way they talked, but they were _different_. They seemed to almost glow with joy and peace.

I took them to the junkyard to look for a part they needed for their stalled-out VW Bug. When we asked about the item, the owner wasn't confident he had it in the vast landscape of car parts and rust.

What happened next caught me totally off-guard. The two guys said to me, "Hey, why don't we agree in prayer and trust Jesus to find the part. After all, He owns this junk yard!" I have to admit I didn't keep my eyes closed. I squinted and looked toward where the owner had been, hoping he hadn't heard the loud declaration that the junkyard belonged to Jesus!

After the amen, one of the guys looked up and said, "Look! There's an old VW engine right over there!" You guessed it. We went over, and the part they needed was on that engine.

I can hear what you might be thinking: Now, wait a minute! I thought God empowered us to do big stuff, really spiritual stuff with lots of God-words and spiritual umph!

Who told you that? Sure, He wants us to do all the things Jesus and His followers did in the Bible. But beyond the so-called "big stuff," He wants to empower us in every aspect of our lives. Power to go to work in the morning. Power to live through depression. Power to love people with different beliefs. Power to lay your hands on the sick and trust God for healing. Power to love your friends, your spouse and your children with a supernatural, limitless love and power to love your enemies. Even power to find things like an engine part.

We are designed to be dependent on something. And, the Holy Spirit wants to be your primary power source.

You probably can imagine how intrigued I was, standing in the junkyard with those two guys. I finally said, "I love Jesus. He's forgiven me, and His Spirit lives in me. I know that's true for you both, but what do you have that I'm missing?" They proceeded to tell me how the Holy Spirit had come *upon* them and filled them with power.

That's what I wanted and what I desperately needed. My life—like my smartphone—had the service connected; I belonged to God; His Spirit lived in me, but I knew I lacked power:

A *full charge*.

It had grown dark by the time we drove back to my house and sat in my driveway talking. The two guys were about to head out on their journey. Before they left, they both laid their hands on me and prayed that I would be filled with the Spirit of God and live by his supernatural power from then on.

I felt nothing. Aren't you supposed to feel something, like maybe an electric shock or a puff of wind? Nothing, nada, nix!

I went inside and went in my bedroom and knelt down and said, "Jesus, I don't know what just happened. I'm actually a bit confused. But one thing I'm not confused about is that I need the power of Your Spirit. I won't stop asking You to fill me, not until I am filled."

As soon as I prayed this prayer, with all the desire and desperation I had in me, something happened. It was as if a blanket was stretched tight above my head and lowered slowly on me. The blanket felt like liquid love. Love as I'd never experienced, with peace slowly moving through my entire body, from my head to my toes.

Then I felt joy. I started to laugh. I'd never been tickled by God; that's the best way I can describe it. Tickled with joy by the Spirit of God who had come upon me! I laughed hard for fifteen minutes. The uncontrollable laughter that only close friends know. Just writing this makes me chuckle right now.

I had just been fully charged and have never been the same since that day. Meeting Jesus had fit me for heaven, experiencing His Spirit's infilling fit me for life.

Just as your smartphone runs on power, so do you and I. Just as your phone needs an initial, full charge, we also need one for our life in God. I found I had a new courage to share my story with others, a new level of love for everyone I encountered and new insight into God's Word. I had power!

And yet, in the same way your phone is constantly being drained as you use it, requiring daily charges, we get drained as we live for God and love others, and we need a continuous connection with the Spirit of God to maintain a fully charged life. Inherently, because of God's grace, you carry the charger with you all the time; however, it's your <u>choice</u> to connect to His power and Life.

What matters is that you stay plugged in.

These verses will show you how God has designed you to function at full capacity only when your power comes from Him.

> But Jesus said, "Someone touched me; I know that **power has gone out** from me."
> Luke 8:46 NIV [emphasis added]

> [Jesus said] Live in me. Make your home in me just as I do in you. In the same way that a branch can't bear grapes by itself but only by being joined [plugged in] to the vine, you can't bear fruit unless you are joined with me. I am the Vine, you are the branches. When you're joined with me and I with you, the relation intimate and organic, the harvest is sure to be abundant. Separated, you can't produce a thing.
> John 15:4–5 MSG

> . . . be filled [plugged in—for any Greek language geeks, this word filled is in the present, active, imperative which means <u>continuously filled</u>] with the Spirit . . .
> Ephesians 5:18 NIV [paraphrase added]

You might be wondering how your life will change when the Spirit comes upon you with power. Let me unpack for you how it often happens and the amazing changes you can expect.

3. SOMETHING HAPPENS WHEN YOU RECEIVE THE SPIRIT'S FULL CHARGE

You might be wondering why the title of this section seems to be so obvious. Well, to many people, it's not. We can be caught off-guard when we have a spiritual experience we've never had before or don't understand fully.

To help you understand how the Spirit often comes upon people—we call this "infilling"—let me start by saying what it doesn't mean:

It doesn't mean that it's always dramatic.

Several accounts in the Bible show the infilling of the Spirit, causing people to speak in a language they've never learned, for example, or to prophesy (which is sharing the heart and thoughts of God).

The Spirit of God's first *full charge* can come in many ways: a weighty peace, tears, laughter, unexplainable joy, a sense of lightness, an overwhelming closeness to God, a hunger for the Bible, a desire to worship God with reckless abandon.

I've observed thousands of people as the Spirit came upon them for the first time. I've noticed that He often does so along the lines of our personalities.

If you tend to be a quieter, more introverted person, you may experience a new peace and confidence. If you are an expressive, extroverted person, you might burst into song, speak a language inspired by God or dance! I've had the privilege of seeing the many ways the Spirit infills a person.

There have been many times I've experienced people falling down under the weightiness of God's presence as it becomes so close. This expression of infilling is often argued about today. It doesn't make sense to us. Falling down, why? But, our ways are not God's ways (Isaiah 55:8,9).

Let me try to explain. People can fall down for several reasons other than tripping. Some fall (faint) from grief. Take, for example, a father I knew whose three-year-old son had drowned. When he saw the boy's body at the funeral home for the first time, the dad was so overcome, he fell to the ground.

Some fall down from joy. Have you ever seen a serviceman or woman return early from a long deployment to surprise their spouse? At times, the couple has to be held up because they lose their strength.

Some fall down from sheer power. How long do you think you

can stand when hit with a taser? Thousands of volts seizing your muscles. I bet not long.

We see several instances in the Bible when people lose their strength because of an encounter with God's holy, awesome and loving presence. Here are a few:

> *It happened that when the priests came from the holy place, the cloud filled the house of the Lord, so that the priests <u>could not stand</u> to minister because of the cloud, for the glory of the Lord filled the house of the Lord.*
> I Kings 8:10–11 NASB [emphasis added]

> *Judas had promised to betray Jesus. So he went to the garden with some Roman soldiers and temple police, who had been sent by the chief priests and the Pharisees. They carried torches, lanterns, and weapons. Jesus already knew everything that was going to happen, but he asked, "Who are you looking for?" They answered, "We are looking for Jesus from Nazareth!" Jesus told them, "I am Jesus!" At once they all backed away and <u>fell to the ground</u>.*
> John 18:4–6 CEV [emphasis added]

> *When I saw him [Jesus], <u>I fell at his feet</u> as if I were dead. But he laid his right hand on me and said, "Don't be afraid! I am the First and the Last. I am*

*the living one. I died, but look—I am alive forever
and ever! And I hold the keys of death and the grave.*
Revelation 1:17–18 NIV [emphasis added]

The Spirit of God will infill each person in a manner He specifically chooses. He always has our best in mind. Count on it.

It doesn't mean it's final.

I can confidently tell you that the Spirit coming upon you, to fully charge you, isn't final at all. His work in us is dynamic and expansive. When people get married, they become one with their spouse. But, with each experience, joy and challenge, they become even more "one."

We can only have one, first full charge, but we can expect to have a lifetime of different charging experiences as we grow in our friendship with Jesus and His Spirit.

I have a friend who struggled to experience the *full charge* of the Spirit. He had asked Jesus; he had people lay hands on him and pray, but he had no assurance that he was filled. As I asked him why he thought that, he answered, "Well, I've never fallen down."

This gave me the chance to show him the many ways the Spirit comes upon us. He began to realize that after he had been prayed for, an unusual peace had descended upon him and stayed with him in spite of great trials he was going through. He was unemployed from a high-paying, executive level job and knew that he should be a giant ball of stress, but wasn't. He knew his life and future were in God's hands and that God would take care of him. He was so "chill" that his wife was concerned for him. It just wasn't like him to be so calm.

She was right. It wasn't like _him_. It was like the Spirit of God.

He realized that he was, indeed, filled. He had a new confidence to seek God for even more of His presence and power. And that God-confidence carried him all the way until God eventually provided the perfect job.

Several months later, he and his wife were talking with their neighbor who had come over to ask them to pray for his daughter. The girl had been very ill and lethargic, too weak to go outside and play. The doctors were at a loss.

In response to this desperate father's request, they laid their hands on the neighbor to pray, and, in an instant, my friend fell to the floor and started speaking a language he had never learned (the Bible calls this speaking in tongues). He continued, non-stop, until the neighbor left, and my friend's wife, quite frustrated, went to bed.

I can only guess as you read this you're like, "I am NEVER going to ask God to fill me! I come across as fairly sane and would like to keep it that way, thank you very much. Who knows what could happen?!" I'm smiling. What could happen is exactly what the Spirit, in His wisdom, wants to happen.

We aren't talking about a tame Spirit, a predictable Spirit or a controllable Spirit. This is the Kingdom of God we're learning about, and this is the Spirit of God! Sometimes He shows up with what I call "orderly chaos!"

The next morning, my friend's wife was like, "What was that all about?!" To which, the man replied, "I don't know." As they tried to process the previous night, movement caught their attention. They looked out the window and saw the neighbor's daughter outside, playing. God had shown up in an unusual way with a supernatural healing.

My friend's initial _full charge_—as evidenced by peace—was far less dramatic than when he was filled again, rambling like crazy on his living room floor. If you stay plugged in by choosing _Him,_ expect the Spirit to fill you progressively, constantly and uniquely.

With the Spirit's infilling,
you can expect supernatural "evidences"

Not only does something happen when God's Spirit fully charges you, but you can also expect to experience many "evidences." Evidence is different from proof.

Proof says, "PROVE IT, AND I'LL BELIEVE."

Evidence says, "I BELIEVE and will continue to thank You with confidence, knowing that the EVIDENCE will come."

There are many "evidences" of the Spirit fully charging a person, but the primary ones are:

Love, Power, Fruitful Living, Supernatural Abilities or Gifts, Purity.

The most important evidence of all is that you will have an increased love for Jesus and for others, especially those who you have a hard time loving...or even liking.

Here are several Scriptures to build your faith as you seek God for the gift of His Spirit.

More Love for God and Others

For we know how dearly God loves us, because he has given us the Holy Spirit to fill our hearts with <u>his</u> love.
    Romans 5:5 NLT [emphasis added]

Three things will last forever—faith, hope, and love—and the <u>greatest of these is love</u>.
    I Corinthians 13:13 NLT [emphasis added]

More Power to Live Out Loud for Jesus

But the Holy Spirit will come upon you and <u>give you power</u>. Then you will tell everyone about me...
    Acts 1:8 CEV [emphasis added]

After they had prayed, the meeting place shook. They were all filled with the Holy Spirit and <u>bravely spoke</u> God's message.

Acts 4:31 CEV [emphasis added]

More of the Fruit, or the Personality of God's Spirit through You

But the Holy Spirit produces this kind of fruit in our lives: love, joy, peace, patience, kindness, goodness, faithfulness, gentleness, and self-control. There is no law against these things! Since we are living by the Spirit, let us follow the Spirit's leading in every part of our lives.

Galatians 5:22–25 NLT

The Release of Supernatural, Spirit-Driven Gifts and Abilities from God

A spiritual gift is given to each of us so we can help each other. To one person the Spirit gives the ability to give wise advice; to another the same Spirit gives a message of special knowledge. The same Spirit gives great faith to another, and to someone else the one Spirit gives the gift of healing. He gives one person the power to perform miracles, and another the ability to prophesy. He gives someone else the ability to discern whether a message is from the Spirit of God or from another spirit. Still another person is given the ability to speak in unknown languages, while another is given the ability to interpret what is being said. It is the one and only Spirit who distributes all these gifts. He alone decides which gift each person should have.

I Corinthians 12:7–11 NLT

More of the Purity of God Experienced in Your Daily Life

At that time the Spirit of the Lord will come powerfully upon you . . . and You will be changed into a different person.

I Samuel 10:6 NLT

So roll up your sleeves, put your mind in gear, be totally ready to receive the gift that's coming when Jesus arrives. Don't lazily slip back into those old grooves of evil, doing just what you feel like doing. You didn't know any better then; you do now. As obedient children, let yourselves be pulled into a way of life shaped by God's life, a life energetic and blazing with holiness. God said, "I am holy; you be holy."

I Peter 1:13–16 MSG

One of the best ways to see the "evidences" is to be around those who are overflowing with the Holy Spirit. They stand out. They aren't bunchy, picky, judgmental Christians. They are humble,

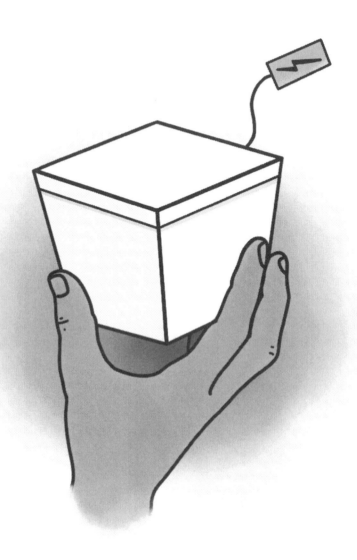

joyful, kind and powerful. You know you're around the Spirit of God on a person when just being with them draws you to love God more, be kinder to yourself and endeavor to serve others even more. His Spirit is contagious.

We've talked a lot about supernatural power from a supernatural Spirit. Can I ask you a question? Since you've given your life to Jesus, have you asked the Spirit to come upon you with power? This experience is God's wonderful gift, and He wants all of those who follow Jesus to have it.

> *"And now I will send the Holy Spirit, just as my Father promised. But stay here in the city until the Holy Spirit comes and fills you with power from heaven."*
> Luke 24:49 NLT

> *Once when he was eating with them, he commanded them, "Do not leave Jerusalem until the Father sends you the gift he promised, as I told you before. John baptized with water, but in just a few days you will be baptized [immersed in] with the Holy Spirit."*
> Acts 1:4–5 NLT [emphasis and paraphrase added]

Did you happen to notice that even though Jesus' disciples had been with Him for three solid years, He didn't want them to do anything for Him until they had been empowered by Him.

— HOW TO BE FULLY CHARGED BY THE HOLY SPIRIT —

Here are some simple steps I hope will help you to experience God's gift to you.

Start by Believing Fully

As much as we want the power of God's Spirit, He wants us to have it all the more. It starts with believing this gift is real and that it's for you.

> [the one] who comes to God must believe that He is, and that He is a rewarder of those who <u>diligently seek</u> Him.
> Hebrews 11:6 NKJV [emphasis added]

Some people have a hard time believing, because they think they aren't worthy to be filled or have to be more spiritual to be filled. This is not true. It is God who made us worthy through the death of His Son and made us heirs of His Kingdom, and the only way we can become more spiritual is through the power of His Spirit.

Be Willing to Seek God Diligently

Once you believe, start to pursue God with a diligence that says, "I have to be filled, I won't stop seeking till I am filled!"

Sometimes the evidence of His coming upon us is immediate, and sometimes it happens only after we have pursued Him with passion. Be assured, He wants you to know, with confidence, that you are filled with the Spirit!

Have you ever been bugged by a three-year-old who really wants something? They are unashamed and relentless in their pursuit—Mom, Mom, Mom, Mom, Mom—until Mom answers. God likes it when we keep asking Him. He likes it when we have the passion of a child.

> *One day Jesus told his disciples a story to show that*
> *they should always pray and never give up.*
> Luke 18:1 NLT

Begin to Ask Expectantly

God promises to grant our request for His Spirit if we ask expectantly. I was trying to describe how this feels to someone, and this image came to mind.

Remember when you were a kid and played the "trusting game"? I don't know if it's called that, but it sounds good.

It was when you would close your eyes and fall backward into the waiting, rescuing arms of the person standing behind you. If you didn't trust your friend or were afraid, you'd find

yourself bending your knees to catch yourself, which made everything awkward. Or, if your friend was ornery, they would step aside, and you would land hard on your tush, hurting you and your pride.

But, when it worked, for a split second, right before you were caught, it was one of the freest, most exhilarating feelings. You decided to "let go" and trust your friend.

God is your Friend. The Spirit is His gift. You can LET GO in your heart as you ask Him to come upon you in power.

> *[Jesus said] And so I tell you, keep on asking, and you will receive what you ask for. Keep on seeking, and you will find. Keep on knocking, and the door will be opened to you. For everyone who asks, receives. Everyone who seeks, finds. And to everyone who knocks, the door will be opened.*
>
> *You fathers—if your children ask for a fish, do you give them a snake instead? Or if they ask for an egg, do you give them a scorpion? Of course not! So if you sinful people know how to give good gifts to your children, how much more will your heavenly Father give the Holy Spirit to those who ask him.*
>
> Luke 11:9–13 NLT [emphasis added]

LIVING WHAT YOU'RE LEARNING

Are you ready to receive God's _fully_ charged gift of His Spirit? You can ask right now, or read through this chapter again until you have a desperation to be filled. Maybe you have questions or want to wait until you can have a friend or someone on the ministry team pray with you. That's okay; just take the next step.

If you've already been fully charged in the past, you can ask God to fill you again!

It's good to think the way a child thinks—hopefully, the way you did when you put your total trust in Jesus. If kids know you have a gift for them, it's the only thing on their minds. They ask and ask for it and won't stop until it's resting in their hands.

If you're ready now, I'm going to lead you in a prayer. I want to encourage you to get alone where there are no distractions. Believe that when you ask, God always hears and will give you the evidence of His Spirit immediately, or progressively.

It may help you to know that, as I write this prayer, I'm asking the Spirit of God to give me the words, and I'm going to pray it out loud as if I were right there with you. Okay, let's say this together.

PRAYER

Dear Jesus, thank you for preparing me for the Gift of the Holy Spirit. You told your disciples to wait for the gift by faith and receive power from heaven.

Here I am, in love with you, wanting to live for you. I choose to lay aside all of my human efforts and ask you for your Spirit's supernatural power to be released in my life with the evidence of more love, power, fruit, gifts and purity. I want to be supernaturally empowered.

I'm asking you with a full heart of anticipation. Fill me with your Holy Spirit! Come upon me with power! I stretch out my spiritual arms and I let go. Fill me now!

(Now wait and be still. Just be there with God. Let me pray for you in this moment: Lord, release your Spirit to my brother or sister who just prayed this, NOW! In Jesus' name. Let's continue out loud.)

Thank you God for hearing my prayer and for fully charging me with Your Spirit!

Teach me to plug in to You with the charging cord of my daily choice.

Have Your way in my life. Use me powerfully for Your Kingdom. In Jesus' Name!

Take a moment to write what you've just experienced while it's fresh, and to thank God for His amazing presence and power.

_____

_____

_____

_____

_____

_____

_____

If you feel like *nothing happened*, like I did after the two hitchhikers prayed for me, don't stop thanking God for hearing your prayer and asking Him to reveal the powerful evidence.

He is faithful; He is filling you.

I'd love to hear what God did as you asked Him to fill you with His Spirit. Touch base with me either via email at: **seniorleadership@discoverlifegate.com** or on my social media accounts. I'd love to hear from and rejoice with you!

CONCLUSION

I hope as you have been reading this last chapter, God has shown you, even more, how much He loves you and wants to provide everything you need in your **brand new** life.

There is so much more in my heart to share about all the amazing things He has in store for you. That's where God's Word, God's Spirit and God's people will fill in the spaces in the days ahead. It's my hope that you've learned many new truths and grown in your love for Jesus as you've read. I pray that you are now more confident and empowered as a follower of Jesus.

This book has been written with you in my heart. It's _for you_. I believe God is working in your life and wants to use you to help others know Him as well.

It has been a blast and blessing to write this on your behalf.

I've included a section at the end with recommended reading to help you, especially in your early growth as a follower of our amazing Jesus.

If this book has helped you, would you share it with someone on their way to knowing Jesus, or with another follower who may benefit from what you've learned?

Let me end by praying blessing on your life:

Dear Jesus,

Thank you for the person holding this book in their hands. I pray they have learned and will continue to learn how to walk as Your **brand new** *creation. May they have a supernatural recollection of the truths they have gained and the decisions they have made.*

I pray you would make them fruitful in all they do. I ask that Your life and love would increase in them with each passing day. Help them grow in joyful obedience to You.
Make them "contagious," so that those in their world may come to know You through their life and words.

Protect them from our adversary and from the temptations and sins he would try endlessly to lure them into. I bind him from their lives in Jesus' mighty name.

Finally, Lord Jesus, I ask You to give them a passion to know You. A passion greater than every other desire in their lives. Fill them over and over with Your power.

Give them unending joy in Your presence, and the confidence that You are always with them and will never leave them. Fill them with Your Peace!

I pray all of these things in Your name, Jesus!

Amen! (So be it! That's what's up!).

RESOURCES TO HELP YOU GROW

I want to recommend the books and the authors listed below. Especially as you are God's **brand new** creation, these resources will help you further understand what God has done for you, and what He wants to continue to do as He transforms you into the person you are destined to become.

The God I Never Knew by Robert Morris
Emotionally Healthy Spirituality by Peter Scazzero
Garden City by John Mark Comer
Love Does by Bob Goff
The Blessed Life by Robert Morris
God Has a Name by John Mark Comer
Heaven by Randy Alcorn
Truly Free by Robert Morris
Victory Over Darkness by Neil Anderson
Jesus Calling by Sara Young
Everybody Always by Bob Goff
The Prodigal God by Timothy Keller
The Next Christian by Gabe Lyons
My Name is Hope by John Mark Comer

BIBLIOGRAPHY

The Four Loves, Copyright © 1960 by C.S. Lewis Pte. Ltd., Published by HarperCollins.

"The Implementation of a Disciple-Making Process in the Local Church" By Eldon Babcock (2002). Doctor of Ministry. Paper 180. http://digitalcommons.georgefox.edu/dmin/180 [Eldon's quote used in this book is an expansion of statements made by Greg Ogden in *The New Reformation,* cited below.]

Merriam-Webster Online Dictionary Copyright © 2015 by Merriam-Webster, Incorporated.

The New Reformation, Copyright © 1990 by Greg Ogden, Published by Zondervan.

The Purpose Driven Life, Copyright © 2002 by Rick Warren, Published by Zondervan.

Made in the USA
San Bernardino,
CA